JAMES
Faith and Works
in Balance

James T. Draper, Jr.

JAMES

Faith and Works
in Balance

Tyndale House
Publishers, Inc.
Wheaton, Illinois

Library of Congress
Catalog Card Number
80-51697
ISBN 0-8423-1852-6, paper
Copyright © 1981
by James T. Draper, Jr.
All rights reserved
First printing, January 1981
Printed in the
United States of America

To Luther Dyer
my friend, beloved and cherished,
whose example and encouragement
have blessed and strengthened me
over many years

CONTENTS

1

Rejoicing
Under
Pressure
James 1:1-4

THE AUTHOR of this biblical book identifies himself as
"James, a servant of God and of the Lord Jesus Christ."
There are at least five men by the name of James who are
mentioned in the New Testament, and at least three have
some prominence in the New Testament writings. But
there is only one James who could have written this book.
He is James, the half-brother of our Lord. Raised in the
same family as Jesus, he was without question the most
outstanding Christian leader of the first century.

The Apostle Paul, John the Apostle, and Simon Peter
were great men. Historically, we have given more prominence to them, but there is no doubt that James was the
premier leader in all of Christendom in the early years of
the Church. Surprisingly, James was apparently not even
saved prior to the crucifixion. It must have been a hard pill
to swallow to see his brother grow up to be the Messiah.
Apparently, James did not accept what Jesus was preaching at the time. But after the resurrection, Jesus made a
special appearance just to James. Whether or not he was
saved then or whether he was saved prior to the appearance of Jesus, we do not know. All of the other post-resur-
rection appearances were to Christians, to believers. But
many believe that this special appearing of Jesus to James
was for the purpose of saving him and calling him into
service.

We perhaps first see James as a Christian when Simon Peter was in jail and the church gathered to pray for him (Acts 12). The Lord answered their prayers, and Peter came to the house where they were praying. Rhoda recognized that it was Simon Peter standing at the door and ran back to the people to tell them, but they did not believe her. "We are praying for him because he is in jail."

"Your prayers have been answered. He has been released," she insisted.

They did not believe it until they opened the door and saw for themselves.

"Go tell James that I have been released," Simon Peter told them.

In A.D. 47, the first real controversy arose in the Church. Judaizers were claiming that to be saved and be a Christian, one had to adhere to all the Old Testament rituals and laws. Others totally disagreed with that position. Paul and his group were representative of this latter group. They believed that salvation was by grace through faith, and that it was not proper to combine Jewish tradition and law with Christian faith. A great controversy arose in the Church, leading to what was known as the first Jerusalem Council. They met in Jerusalem to debate the issue and to determine what would be accepted as truth. James presided at that meeting; James rendered the verdict; James made the authoritative statement that was issued to the churches and to the apostles. James, without any question, was the most outstanding, most influential leader in the early Christian Church.

We might think that a man of this prestige would introduce himself as "James, the half-brother of our Lord," or "James, the presider of the leaders of the church of Jerusalem." But instead he simply says, "James, a servant of God and of the Lord Jesus Christ." This is the only place in the New Testament that this particular description is

JAMES
1:1-4
not coupled with another descriptive phrase (for example, "Paul, a servant and an apostle," or "Paul, a servant called to be an apostle"). But James simply says, "a servant." This is the Greek word *doulos*, "bondslave." He identifies himself in terms that leave no question as to where the glory is to be given. This reference to himself gave complete honor and glory to Jesus Christ. He claimed to be simply a servant of Christ.

Here we see the humility that ought to characterize our lives. The Apostle Paul said, "Who am I, and who is Apollos, that we should be the cause of a quarrel? Why, we're just God's servants, each of us with certain special abilities, and with our help you believed. My work was to plant the seed in your hearts, and Apollos' work was to water it, but it was God, not we, who made the garden grow in your hearts. The person who does the planting or watering isn't very important, but God is important because he is the one who makes things grow" (1 Corinthians 3:5-7). At the end of that chapter, he talks about the fact that the honor does not belong to Paul or to Apollos or Cephas, but to Jesus Christ.

James simply identified himself as a man obligated to give absolute obedience, absolute loyalty to Jesus Christ. *Doulos* was used in the Septuagint to refer to all of the prophets and all of the great men of the Old Testament. They described themselves as "servants of Yahweh," "servants of Jehovah."

When James said, "I am a servant," he was saying, "As one of a long line of people who have given their lives to Christ, I now declare to you the word of God."

"From: James, a servant of God and of the Lord Jesus Christ. To: Jewish Christians scattered everywhere. Greetings! Dear brothers, is your life full of difficulties and temptations? Then be happy, for when the way is rough, your patience has a chance to grow. So let it grow, and don't try to squirm out of your problems. For when your patience is finally in full bloom, then you will be ready for anything, strong in character, full and complete" (James 1:1-4).

THE DESTINATION

James says, "... to the twelve tribes which are scattered abroad" (KJV), obviously addressing the twelve tribes of the dispersion, but also the dispersion of Christians in the first century. He is not talking about Israel, but rather the Christian church which, according to Paul, had become the true Israel (Romans 4).

"Twelve tribes" indicates a unit, but how can a unit be scattered? James is saying that even though circumstances forced the Christians to be torn apart physically, they were still one in the grace of God. They were scattered abroad, yet together as God's people.

Nothing that happens to us takes us out of the care of God. Nothing removes us from his concern for our lives. No matter how dark the valley, God will see us through it. Thus, James immediately begins to talk about the trials and testings that come into everyone's life. It is as though James is saying, "You twelve tribes have been scattered abroad, but God knows where every single one of you is. He has his eye upon you."

"Greetings" was the usual secular greeting rather than the typical opening Paul always used. Paul would say, "Grace and peace be unto you." James just says, "Greetings." Properly translated it simply means "rejoice." "I am writing this, a servant of God in the Lord Jesus Christ, to those of you who are scattered abroad, but are still one in the mind and heart of God. Rejoice in your circumstances."

He goes on, "dear brothers." Through Jesus Christ, we

are brothers and sisters, and we need to cultivate that relationship. We belong to the same Lord, we have a common heritage, a common origin. Throughout this book we will see a tremendous emphasis on love, fellowship, and compassion for each other.

There are two aspects of this letter that we will be considering: the pressures believers were to bear, and their faithfulness under pressure. This group of people had some problems. They had a problem of giving deference to wealthy people and of not having compassion for the poor. They had a problem with talking too much. James does not overlook this. This message from James is not a theological treatise. He tells us how to live. He tells us how to get dressed in the morning, how to go to work, how to relate to people around us. He is not as concerned with doctrine as he is with performance. He is concerned that we who say, "I belong to Christ, I believe in him," have a life that says the same thing. That is the thrust of this striking letter.

THE DISCIPLINE

"Dear brothers, is your life full of difficulties and temptations? Then be happy, for when the way is rough, your patience has a chance to grow" (1:2, 3). "Temptations" rightly means "testing." We usually think of temptation as something that Satan does to try to get us to do wrong, something designed to make us sin. But this word means more than that. God may allow Satan, as he did with Job, to make some attacks upon our lives. But temptation may also include things which God may bring into our lives to test our faith. It is a word which means, "to test with a desire to see the quality of the object tested."

The Greek verb which is the root of this word was used of a young bird "testing" its wings. Testing is not meant to make me fall, but to make me fly; not to make me stumble, but to make me stand; not to defeat me, but to cause me to rise victoriously. The goal of God's testing is to strengthen, to give victory rather than defeat.

Notice some things about God's discipline. First, he says, "be happy" or "count it all joy" (KJV). He did not say that the trials were a joy or happiness, but that when we have testings and trials, we should consider it a joy. In other words, look on the bright side of it. God is in control; he will bring victory out of it. He is allowing a test of our faith in order to produce a stronger faith. He is conducting a test of our lives so we can stand strong and secure, so we can face life with confidence. We can look at trials like that with joy, because we know that God's desired result will come to pass.

He says, "count it all joy *when* you fall into divers temptations" (KJV), not *if*. We can't choose whether or not we will fall into testing. We will be tested. God sees to it. If we think for a minute that when we get "spiritual," we will stop being tested, we are mistaken. God is always in the process of testing his children. Read Genesis 22, where God tells Abraham to sacrifice Isaac. When Abraham raised the knife to slay his son as a sacrifice upon the altar, God said, "Stop; I just wanted to see if you would withhold your son from me. I was testing you." Testing comes to all of us.

Paul said, " . . . what persecutions I endured: but out of them all the Lord delivered me" (2 Timothy 3:11, KJV). He did not say that God delivered him "from" them, but "out of them." God wants us to have victory in the midst of trouble. "Count it all joy when you enter into testing."

Notice that James says, "when you *fall* into . . ." This is the same word used to describe the man who traveled from Jerusalem to Jericho and "fell" among thieves (Luke 10:30). The crime was very unexpected; it happened suddenly. Most problems come like that. If we knew we were going to have a problem, we would avoid it. God says, "Count it all joy when you suddenly and unexpectedly fall into various testings." We must not let the nature of our circumstances or the swiftness with which trials often come cause us to lose heart.

The word "divers" (KJV) is a word which means "different kinds," "a great variety." In other words, it doesn't matter what kind of trial, testing, or difficulty we fall into. We are to rejoice and be happy in all of them. Whatever trial or problem we face, this word includes it.

THE DETERMINATION

"... for when the way is rough, your patience has a chance to grow. So let it grow, and don't try to squirm out of your problems. For when your patience is finally in full bloom, then you will be ready for anything, strong in character, full and complete" (1:3, 4).

"Trying" (KJV) could be translated "purging." When a precious metal is heated until it is liquid and the impurities rise to the top so they can be scraped off, it has been purged. Another example is the smelting of steel or iron when it is heated and all the impurities removed so that what is left is pure metal. The cooled, set metal will be strong and sturdy. That is the word used here. It means to purge so as to purify and strengthen. The "trying" of our faith develops patience.

"Patience" is one of those English words that has greatly changed in meaning. Going well beyond what our idea of patience conveys, it means "endurance." The trying of our faith will result in great endurance on our part. We will stand strong. We will be victorious. We will gain confidence, boldness, victory.

But wait a moment—we have all known people who have grown *impatient* under testing. Is James saying that

15

testing always works patience? Yes, if we couple it with verse 4: "For when your patience is finally in full bloom...." The word "perfect" (KJV) or "full bloom" means to bring to completion, to fulfill the purpose for which it was created. Patience is always the result when our faith is tested *if* we let the test run its course.

Have you ever taught a child how to ride a bicycle? He fell a few times, right? He would never learn how to ride if we didn't let go of the bicycle, just as a child would have a very difficult time learning how to walk if we never let go of his hand. God is telling us to let our testing run its course. He wants us to lay our problems at the foot of the cross and let him do his work in our lives. In God's time, when the test is completed, our lives will demonstrate an enduring, steadfast patience. Then we "will be ready for anything, strong in character, full and complete." That is what comes from facing trials and testing with determination.

Never accuse God of not knowing what is happening. Nothing comes to us that does not come by his permissive will. He knows every disappointment, every point of pressure. James is saying, "I know what it is like to have heartaches, to face pressure. Whatever trials or testings come into your life, regardless of how they appear, let God have his way in you. When the testing is finished, it will have produced in you a pure faith that is strong and sturdy. Victory will be yours, and you will be complete."

God brought qualities into my life that never would have been brought had I not experienced the sorrow and bereavement of my father's death. I learned something I could have never learned any other way. Testing perfects us. Points of pressure brought to bear on us are God's tools. Testing, trials, troubles are God's pruning shears, his purging fire, his carpenter's bench in order to make us what we need to be.

2

The Wisdom for Trials
James 1:5-8

AFTER THE ADMONITION to be happy when we enter into various testings, James now points us to wisdom for such testing. "If you want to know what God wants you to do, ask him, and he will gladly tell you, for he is always ready to give a bountiful supply of wisdom to all who ask him; he will not resent it. But when you ask him, be sure that you really expect him to tell you, for a doubtful mind will be as unsettled as a wave of the sea that is driven and tossed by the wind; and every decision you then make will be uncertain, as you turn first this way, and then that. If you don't ask with faith, don't expect the Lord to give you any solid answer" (1:5-8).

It is not normal to react to pressures by being happy about them. We need a special kind of wisdom to act like that. Thus James quickly adds, "If you lack wisdom, ask God for it, who will give liberally." The wisdom he speaks of here is not merely information, or simply education, nor indeed is it training. The wisdom spoken of here is the ability to judge and evaluate sorrow and joy from God's standpoint, to view from God's perspective what comfort and pain mean, understanding wealth and poverty on a divine level.

If we look strictly from man's perspective, we will not respond in a godly way to the pressures that these bring upon us. This wisdom is the ability to know that in the midst of everything, God will work out that which is best for us, that no experience will defeat us or separate us from his love. We can know that "all things work together for good to them that love God, to them who are the called according to his purpose" (Romans 8:28, KJV).

This will change our attitudes. Suppose we have an unreasonable employer who is driving us crazy. We are unhappy in our job. We are under immense pressure. He doesn't understand us or help us. If we look at that from man's wisdom, all we get is confusion and irritation. But if we look at it with the wisdom of God, we may see that employer as a tool of God to bring a godly temperament into our lives.

Or suppose someone has wronged us or criticized us unjustly. We have been greatly hurt. We might recoil in anger and bitterness. That is what human wisdom would say we should do. But if we respond in godly wisdom, we would see in that wrong and in the hurtful attitude of that person toward us an opportunity to put into practice the precept of our Lord: "Bless them that curse you, and pray for them which despitefully use you" (Luke 6:28, KJV).

If we realize that in every relationship and every responsibility we are serving God, that our relationship to him is expressed in how we discharge those responsibilities, then rather than reacting negatively and with hostility we will react in a positive way, knowing that we are doing that work as unto the Lord.

Do we find ourselves losing some money through a bad investment? If tremendous discouragement and depression are settling in upon us, we have earthly wisdom. It could be that God's wisdom would say to us that this is his way of showing us not to trust in uncertain riches, not to put our treasures and our hearts in the wrong places.

Whatever form our trial takes, we are to count it all joy.

We need to see that the most important thing is not for us to have prosperity and ease, but to be better men and women. It is not important simply to have the things we want to have, but to be righteous before God and to walk in his holiness. When we see this as the top priority, it will change and broaden the whole horizon of life.

There is no limit to what God can do. If we view material things only from a human standpoint, life is bound by the limit of our possessions, by the stretching of our dollars, by the things which we call our own. If we view the success of our families or friendships simply by whether or not everyone is content and cooperative, then the moment one person steps out of line or one misunderstanding arises, it destroys the whole relationship. We will find our lives fenced in, with every little circumstance transforming what could be a happy life into absolute misery. But if we have the wisdom James is talking about, there is no limit to what God can achieve through our circumstances. Every pressure becomes an opportunity. Every disappointment becomes a chance for God to perform a miracle in our lives. Rather than being a tragedy when disappointment comes or rather than being in despair when discouragement hits us, we face opportunities for God to operate in a new level in our lives.

We need God's wisdom. An exasperated man will do unwise things. A person who is distraught will not make good choices. A man who is upset will make foolish decisions. When James says, "If any of you lack wisdom" (KJV), he is not indicating that some of us may not lack it. We all lack this kind of wisdom, because human reason is just not sufficient for what we need. One of the most amazing things I have found in studying this matter of human wisdom was in 1 Samuel. "And David behaved himself wisely in all his ways; and the Lord was with him. Wherefore when Saul saw that he behaved himself very wisely, he was afraid of him" (18:14, 15, KJV). Saul had tried to kill David, but rather than responding with hostility and anger, he behaved himself wisely and Saul became fearful.

When God asked Solomon, "What can I give to you?" Solomon answered, "Give me an understanding mind so that I can govern your people well and know the difference between what is right and what is wrong" (1 Kings 3:9). Wisdom was the cry of his heart.

The book of Proverbs, devoted to the pursuit of wisdom, describes and defines wisdom as the ability to live in a fashion that is pleasing to God. We need that kind of wisdom. The natural man doesn't have it (1 Corinthians 2:14). Job tells us that even age does not bring the kind of wisdom that we must have to face the perplexity of life. Every one of us would have to say that when there has been pressure, discouragement, disappointment, we have needed a special kind of wisdom to deal with it.

THE SOURCE OF WISDOM
"If you want to know what God wants you to do, ask him, and he will gladly tell you, for he is always ready to give a bountiful supply of wisdom to all who ask him; he will not resent it" (1:5). We cannot get such wisdom by going to school. We do not get it by experience. We do not get it by enduring trials. It is a gift of God. Unless we ask God for it, we will never have this kind of wisdom.

All of us desire to do better. We react badly to pressure and determine not to react that way again, but we do. The only way to have the kind of balance and power that comes from God's wisdom is to ask him for it. There is tremendous power in prayer. If we desire wisdom, we must ask God for it.

James says three things about God. First: "He giveth to all men" (1:5, KJV). It is God's nature to give. The lost

man views God as having a clenched fist; the saved man
knows God has an open hand. God gives! The very life
that we have is the fruit of God's concern for us. "For he
maketh his sun to rise on the evil and on the good, and
sendeth rain on the just and on the unjust" (Matthew
5:45, KJV). God is a giving God. So we can ask God for
wisdom confidently, because we know God wants to give
it to us. "He is always ready to give a bountiful supply"
(1:5). A generous man is a happy man because he is most
like God; a stingy man is always unhappy.

"Bountiful" just means "generous." God is not stingy.
He always gives us more than we ask. He always gives
abundantly—"good measure, pressed down, and shaken
together, and running over" (Luke 6:38, KJV). We may
ask for wisdom in one particular situation, but God, who
gives generously, will respond with a wisdom that blesses
the whole horizon of our lives.

"He will not resent it" (1:5). That simply means that
God does not give us something and then condemn us
because we asked for it. He does not give us something
and then say, "You ask too much." God is always glad to
give to us.

SECURING THIS WISDOM
How do we get this kind of wisdom from God? By asking
him for it! "It shall be given him" (1:5, KJV). That is an
absolute certainty. If we need wisdom for any choice or
any decision, we simply have to ask for it. If we ask, we
will receive it.

We may say, "I have asked God for wisdom and I am
still confused." Well, James deals with that too. "But
when you ask him, be sure that you really expect him to
tell you, for a doubtful mind will be as unsettled as a wave
of the sea that is driven and tossed by the wind" (1:6). The

21

prayer that brings God's wisdom is the prayer that is wrapped up in faith. Notice that he did not say to ask "with" faith. We have the idea that faith is sort of an addendum, a coat that we put on, something that we add to our prayers. But James said, "ask *in* faith" (KJV).

In other words, the prayers that come from our heart should come from a heart of faith. "He that cometh to God must believe that he is" (Hebrews 11:6, KJV). Faith is a conscious response of our hearts to God, so that when we pray we don't have to say, "By the way, Lord, I believe you are going to do it." We pray "out of faith." We pray "in" faith in God. When God is at the center of our lives, when life revolves around him and faith is the atmosphere of our lives, then our prayers come not along *with* faith, but out of the midst of faith.

If we want this kind of wisdom, we must ask in faith. "Whatsoever is not of faith is sin" (Romans 14:23, KJV). If there is any area of our lives that is not consistent with our faith in God, then it is sinful and keeps us from praying in faith. There are many of us who seem to think we can live like the Devil but still get what we want from God. If there are areas of disobedience, if we contradict what he tells us to do, if we are not patterning our life according to the Word of God, then we are not praying in faith. If we ask God for wisdom but still have confusion in our minds, it is because there is sin in our lives.

"But when you ask him, be sure that you really expect him to tell you, for a doubtful mind will be as unsettled as a wave of the sea that is driven and tossed by the wind; and every decision you then make will be uncertain, as you turn first this way, and then that. If you don't ask with faith, don't expect the Lord to give you any solid answer" (1:6, 7). A man who does not pray out of faith is a wavering man, unstable in all of his ways. He is fickle. His devotion is high and then low. He is hot and then cold. That kind of person is tossed by every wind that comes along. Every pressure that is brought to bear upon his life will bear fruits of confusion and despair. A man who prays out of anything but faith is just like that. God never intended for us to live like that.

"If you don't ask with faith, don't expect the Lord to give you any solid answer" (1:8). We cannot know God's peace and happiness if wavering is the pattern of our lives. There is no possibility of God giving us wisdom if that is the way we are.

"A double-minded man is unstable in all his ways" (1:8, KJV). The word translated double-minded appears only twice in the New Testament and literally means "two-souled." He is a man with two affections. He is trying to serve two masters, trying to love God and Satan at the same time. He is trying to love both spiritual things and sinful things. He is destroyed and torn apart because he is a "double-minded" man.

Such a man is unstable in all of his ways. A man or woman who cannot pray out of faith and who is unstable in his relationship with God is unstable in everything he does—his home, his business, his friendships. A person pulled in two different directions spiritually will be that way in every other area of life. Do we find ourselves unstable in business, unsettled at home, unsteady in our relationships in society? It is a dead giveaway that we are unstable in our relationship with God.

Now we can see why it is so important for us to have God's wisdom in our lives. We thought it was just a matter of making spiritual choices and decisions, but we need God's wisdom not only to enable us to respond to God's call, but to maintain all our relationships in a stable, constant manner. If we are having difficulty in some area of our lives, the root cause involves our relationship with God. If we are walking in right relationship to God, then all other relationships will be right.

How important it is to walk with God every day! The

preceding passage says, "*When* you enter into various testings...." We *will* enter into them. Pressures *will* rise. Disappointments *will* come. How much we need God's wisdom so we can face it all in his power.

3

The Poor
Rich Man
James 1:9-11

"A CHRISTIAN who doesn't amount to much in this world should be glad, for he is great in the Lord's sight. But a rich man should be glad that his riches mean nothing to the Lord, for he will soon be gone, like a flower that has lost its beauty and fades away, withered—killed by the scorching summer sun. So it is with rich men. They will soon die and leave behind all their busy activities" (1:9-11).

James declares that we can be tested in many ways. One way is the test of poverty. Another is wealth.

The last chapter talked about the double-minded man who was unstable in everything. Such a man has the wrong view of life. He thinks that if he is poor, he is forsaken of God and if he is wealthy, he is blessed of God. James proceeds to tell us how we really ought to think. "A Christian who doesn't amount to much in this world should be glad." "Doesn't amount to much" comes from a word that could be translated "undistinguished." It refers to someone who seems to be of no importance, someone who is poor or has no apparent value in the community. It is incredible to think this kind of man should be happy. We think we ought to rejoice when we win honors, when we are popular or have the possessions we want. But James encourages the man who is undistinguished to rejoice, because he is exalted in God's sight.

He seems to be poor, but he is rich. Let that man rejoice! In other words, poverty is not what it seems to be. A man's life does not consist in the abundance of things he possesses. To please God is to be rich, spiritually.

Now for the flipside. The man who is wealthy in the things of this world should rejoice that his personal value is more permanent than his wealth. A man who is wealthy has equal value with the man who is poor.

Remember when Samuel went to anoint a new king? God sent Samuel to the house of Jesse. The sons of Jesse came before the prophet and the first one, Eliab, was a tall, handsome, striking young man. Samuel spontaneously said, "Surely this is the one God wants. He has everything a leader ought to have." But God said, "He is not the one; I have rejected him. Man sees only the outward appearance, but I look upon the heart." Man judges in one way; God judges in another way.

A NEW PERSPECTIVE
Today we look upon being undistinguished or poor as a mark of shame. But James gives us a new perspective. We will be tested many times by the lack of the things we desire to have in this life, whether material possessions, the acclaim of our peers, or the friendship of those about us. But the man of low degree is exalted, being of great worth.

He matters in the church, for in the church he stands on equal footing with everyone there. He is a joint-heir with God and Christ. Someday he will live and reign with Christ, along with all other believers.

He matters in the world because God declares, "I have a purpose and a direction for your life. I have something for you to do, something for you to be. You matter to me. I have a plan for your life." He matters in the world because he matters to God. He learns that he is precious in the sight of God. The man of low degree can rejoice because he is an individual of tremendous worth to God.

If we don't have the money we want or the physical possessions we desire to have, we view our situation as tragic. But God says, "The sufferings of this present time are not worthy to be compared with the glory which shall be revealed in us" (Romans 8:18, KJV). And, "For our light affliction, which is but for a moment, worketh for us a far more exceeding and eternal weight of glory; while we look not at the things which are seen, but at the things which are not seen: for the things which are seen are temporal; but the things which are not seen are eternal" (2 Corinthians 4:17, 18, KJV). God is saying that poverty and hardship are not what they seem to be.

The greatest temptation the poor face is coveteousness. We would think that the rich would be the most coveteous, but it is easy for those who do not have all the things they would like to have to view themselves as deprived. "And the cares of this world, and the deceitfulness of riches, and the lusts of other things entering in, choke the word, and it becometh unfruitful" (Mark 4:19, KJV). Jesus says, "Riches are deceitful." They are not what they seem to be. When we give ourselves to acquire material and physical things, we find that we have received less than we thought we were getting. It just doesn't satisfy.

James is saying, "Don't become bitter and depressed by dwelling on your poverty, but recognize from a new perspective that you are exalted in the eyes of God and in the face of eternity." There is no room in the Christian's life for bitterness because we don't have what we want. We would then be saying that God has given us less than we need.

On the other hand, there is no room for the brother who is low to rejoice in his exaltation and "lord it over others" or to have spiritual pride. "Be glad" means "to exalt." It is a joy that is inwardly felt and outwardly expressed in the individual's life, but it is not arrogance.

Most of us are tested at the point of poverty; but a few are tested at the point of riches. "But a rich man should be glad that his riches mean nothing to the Lord." Most rich folk gauge their lives on what they can see, feel, hear, and touch, on their bank accounts and possessions. James is telling the rich not to rejoice in uncertain riches, that which is unstable. A man who has material possessions—and we in America have an abundance of this world's goods— has a false sense of security. He easily trusts in those things that are fleeting and temporary. "But a rich man should be glad that his riches mean nothing to the Lord, for he will soon be gone, like a flower that has lost its beauty and fades away, withered—killed by the scorching summer sun. So it is with rich men. They will soon die and leave behind all their busy activities" (1:10, 11).

In other words, his value is not in his possessions, not in the things that he has, not in the acclaim of those around him. His value, like the poor man, is that which is his through God.

A rich man is likely to think of himself more highly than he ought. He is likely to think that because he has some of the material things of this world, he is somebody. The saddest thing we can think of is for a rich man to wake up some morning and find that his money is all that he is worth. A man who depends solely on riches will go through all of his lifetime never knowing whether his friends are friends because of what he has or because of what he is.

The rich man is to rejoice not in what he possesses, but in what he is through Jesus Christ. Christianity is the great equalizer. Nobody is poor in God's kingdom. We are equal before God.

We have a tendency to rejoice about the wrong things. Remember when Jesus sent the seventy out and they came back rejoicing because the demons were subject to them.

They were excited over their power. Jesus told them not to rejoice that the demons were subject to them, but to rejoice rather that their names were written down in heaven (Luke 10:17-20).

We get more excited about what we possess than we do about who possesses us. Before God everyone is significant and important, not on the basis of what we have, but because we are in Jesus Christ.

A NEW POSITION

Notice that the poor man is exalted and the rich man is made low. Peter describes this in terms of an inheritance: "And God has reserved for his children the priceless gift of eternal life; it is kept in heaven for you, pure and undefiled, beyond the reach of change and decay" (1 Peter 1:4). And John records Christ's words to the church in Smyrna, "I know how much you suffer for the Lord, and I know all about your poverty (but you have heavenly riches!)" (Revelation 2:9).

We have a new position in Jesus Christ. When tempted to be bitter, envious, to rise in resentment against those around us and even sometimes against God, remember that we are not beggars; we are kings and princes with Jesus Christ. We have been placed in heavenly places. We are children of the King. If we would keep our thoughts upon the palaces that are being prepared for us through Christ Jesus, upon the crowns that already belong to us, upon the dignity that we will win by being gracious and tender, what a difference it would make. How tragic when we live beneath our position. There is no reason for the compromise and the apathy, the hostilities and the anger that characterize so many of God's children.

We are now heirs of God, and everything that God possesses is ours. Our earthly condition may seem desperate at times. Our physical well-being may be critical at points. But every moment we live, God's heaven is hanging over our heads. Every promise of divine love is ours.

The rich also have a new position to rejoice in—they are made low. James is simply saying to us that just as poverty is not what it seems to be, wealth is not what it seems to be either. Nothing we can possess can satisfy us. Most suicides are by wealthy people. What they have does not give them joy. When asked how much money it takes to make a man happy, John D. Rockefeller answered, "Just a little more."

No man is ever lifted up because of what he does. Our righteousness is as filthy rags in the sight of God. Nothing we can do can commend us to him. So, in being brought low, we can actually be exalted with Christ eternally.

Peter talks about this matter of our position: "Being born again, not of corruptible seed, but of incorruptible, by the Word of God, which liveth and abideth for ever. For all flesh is as grass, and all the glory of man as the flower of grass. The grass withereth, and the flower thereof falleth away: but the word of the Lord endureth for ever" (1 Peter 1:23-25a, KJV). As believers, we are eternally secure in Christ.

A NEW PERMANENCE

"But a rich man should be glad that his riches mean nothing to the Lord, for he will soon be gone, like a flower that has lost its beauty and fades away, withered—killed by the scorching summer sun. So it is with rich men. They will soon die and leave behind all their busy activities" (1:10, 11). This is based on Isaiah 40:6-8. It is a reminder to us of the uncertain riches this world possesses.

James used an example that would be very dramatic for the people in the Holy Land. In the desert places, when rain would come, the shoots of grass would appear almost immediately out of the barren, dusty soil and would begin to make their way up. But then the wind from the southeast would blow across the desert. It would blow from the desert with the breath of hot air like a smoldering oven. Literally in a matter of moments it would wither everything in sight.

James declares that this world's wealth is like that. As quickly as the wind would blow off the desert and cause the plants to die, that is how quickly riches can be gone. Don't trust in that which is so temporal. We must not trust in our bank accounts; they can disappear in a moment. We cannot trust our health. We dare not trust the applause of men. This world is fickle, and the applause of men quickly turns sour. These are all uncertain riches.

It is amazing that we spend so much of our time trying to get that which we can't keep, that which won't satisfy us. "So also shall the rich man fade away in his ways" (KJV). "In his ways" literally means "in his goings or journeyings." The man who depends on the material things of this world will one day fade away. It will all be over, and everything that he trusts will be gone.

After you have worked all your life to accumulate all that you could, and you die, whose will those things be that you worked so hard for? What are you going to leave your family that is worth having? Riches can fade away, health can be gone, and a good name can disappear in a moment. It is only as a man has a true perspective of riches that he can really know what life is all about.

We see two men in this passage: the poor rich man, rich in this world's goods, but poor if that is all he possesses; and the rich poor man, poor in this world's possessions, but rich eternally. May we not sink our lives in that which fades away, but lay hold on that which is eternal through Jesus Christ. Real wealth lies in him.

A Crown
of Life
James 1:12

"HAPPY IS THE MAN who doesn't give in and do wrong when he is tempted, for afterwards he will get as his reward the crown of life that God has promised those who love him" (1:12).

The word "happy" jumps out at us. It was used in many of the Psalms of David. The King James Version translates it "blessed," and it was a key word in the Lord's introduction to his Sermon on the Mount. It speaks of prosperity, fulfillment, and goodness for our lives. "Blessed or happy is the man who endures temptation."

AN UNNATURAL RESPONSE

Happiness is not a normal response to temptation and testing. We would say, "Blessed is the man who is never under pressure. Blessed is the one who never has his faith tested. Blessed is the individual who always gets his way, who is prosperous, who never experiences sorrow, who never knows sickness, who always succeeds."

The word "happy" could be translated "fortunate" or "prosperous." The person who experiences this happiness is better off for having experienced it. He is a fortunate person. This happiness is not to be confused with human happiness, which is so dependent upon circumstances. The English word "happiness" comes from an old Scandinavian word that literally means "whatever happens to happen." So, if things happen to happen well, then we are happy. That is the way we normally view life. But God tells us here that when he views our testing and trial, he concludes that we are very fortunate indeed.

I have heard some say to individuals under pressure, "God must love you a lot to allow so much to come upon you." Every experience, every trial of life, every disappointment, every point of pressure is an opportunity for God to reveal his power in our lives. If we never experience trial, we would never know that God can relieve the pressure, that he can lift us above the trial. The great tragedy in many Christians today is that we walk on such a low level that we are never aware of the intervention of God in our lives.

James is speaking about trials, not the temptation to do evil. For he says, "Blessed is the man that *endureth* temptation" (KJV). We don't endure enticement to do evil; we resist it and overcome it. James is not talking about inner temptation to do evil, but about outward circumstances. When we endure the testing of our faith, we are blessed and happy indeed. That is an amazing response to testing.

The words "doesn't give in" is the verb form of the word translated "patience" in verses 3 and 4. He is not encouraging us to "tough" it out or just to grin and bear it. There has to be a better way than that! "Patience" means steadfast endurance, standing strong in God's wisdom and with God's power in our lives. Happy is the man who doesn't just simply go through testing, but endures it. His endurance has the capacity to take something that could devastate him, turn it around and make it into a blessing, a victory. ~~It is the right attitude toward God that enables his Spirit to work in us and transmute trials into victory.~~

AN UNCOMPROMISING VERDICT

"For when he is ~~tried . . .~~" (KJV). The word "tried" is translated in more recent translations, ~~"when he is approved."~~ It is the Greek word meaning to test metal to see if ~~it is pure, to purge~~ out the impurities and leave only the purest metal. The word speaks of heating a piece of metal in the furnace in order to scrape off the impurities that rise to the top. What is left is pure and valuable. ~~The testings and pressures of life are God's ways of testing our characters.~~ We are approved; then we receive the crown of life. If there is no testing, there can be no reward, no victory, no blessing. Testing is God's way of proving the value of our faith and of our lives.

If we come through the testing and are not approved, there is no worthy metal in us at all. If we are beaten into submission by our circumstances, this shows our worthlessness. Circumstances are designed not to beat us into submission, not to destroy our faith, but to reveal its purity and increase its strength. ~~When we go through the testing times of life, God is removing the impurities from us.~~ God is taking from our lives that which is unworthy. He is removing that which is carnal, taking from our hearts that which is impure, so that he can reveal and approve that which is left.

~~If only the greatest desire of our hearts were to be approved of God! We want to be approved of each other, but here we learn that the testings of life come our way in order that we may be approved by God.~~ If we would spend the same energy, the same determination, the same dedication seeking to be approved of God as we do being approved of those around us, what a difference it would make in our lives. And when we are approved, we will receive the crown of life which God has promised to us.

AN UNPARALLELED GIFT

Now we see a gift which is unprecedented. It is almost unfathomable, unbelievable. It is a promise beyond our wildest imaginations. We shall receive "the crown of life."

These folks James is writing to would understand the crown. It had been a prominent part of ancient history. The crown took many forms. Most of the time, it was simply one made of leaves, branches, or perhaps a simple band of cloth. Of course, we are familiar with crowns made of precious metal such as gold and sometimes with precious gems studding the crown, but the crown was not just used by kings. It was worn for many different occasions and for many different purposes. Sometimes those seeking protection would wear a crown and the crown would be a demonstration of trust for salvation and protection. Those who had achieved high acclaim in the world would have a crown placed upon their heads. It was a sign of victory in the Olympic Games and other athletic competition. It was a sign of joy and happiness. It was a sign of freedom. Ancient manuscripts tell about Israelite slaves who when they were freed wore crowns upon their heads to show their freedom.

When we come into biblical times, and in particular, New Testament times, we find that the crown was a victor's crown. Often the Apostle Paul would refer to the crown of conquest and the crown of victory. Paul talks about the church and the believers in Thessalonica being his crown of joy. "What is our crown of rejoicing? Are not even ye? . . . ye are our glory and joy" (1 Thessalonians 2:19, 20, KJV).

It was also a crown of life. In writing to the church at

Ephesus, John mentioned a "tree of life" (Revelation 2:7). Just as the ancients would pluck leaves and branches from the trees for the crowns, so the crown of life is plucked from the tree of life. Then it is placed on the heads of God's children as a gift from God. It is a crown that death can never snatch away. Indeed, from the construction of the language, the crown *is* life, a living crown.

This means more than life in eternity. It is a quality of life we can enjoy now. Jesus called it abundant life. When we go through the testing's fire, we will receive the crown of abundant life.

A crown represents something done or something achieved. The crown of life is evidence of a completed work of grace in our hearts. God will say, "Well done, thou good and faithful servant." This crown means joy and happiness, victory and salvation, protection and honor. It means all of the things that we associate with the use of crowns in ancient times, and more.

Everything in this life loses its value to us. Everything the world gives wears out. It grows old in our mind. But this is a living crown. What Jesus gives us is best today and better tomorrow. Every human acclaim, every human achievement, every human blessing goes downhill. But every day with Jesus is sweeter than the day before. The longer we serve him, the sweeter he grows.

If we have been saved over a long period of time but our faith is not more precious to us today than it was when we were saved, we are living beneath our privilege. We are living beneath what God wants us to live. God wants us to walk with him in joy, with the crown of life adorning our brows and with victory and joy accompanying our steps day by day, so that Christ grows more precious and sweet to us every day.

Maybe we have reacted to the testing times of life with bitterness and hostility, poisoning our own soul. We have poisoned the wellsprings of our own lives. Maybe that is why our faith is not as precious to us now as once it was. Or maybe we have depended on our own energies, our bank accounts, our talents, our abilities and have never really given God a chance to prove that he can be sufficient in our lives.

God has promised to give us the crown of life if we endure testing. There are many things we promise each other, but what God promises, God delivers. When we face testing with steadfast endurance that rises victoriously over it, God guarantees us the crown of life.

AN UNAVOIDABLE CONDITION

"Happy is the man who doesn't give in and do wrong when he is tempted, for afterwards he will get as his reward the crown of life that God has promised those who love him" (1:12). There is a condition to receiving the blessings of God. That is not to say that we must do something and thus deserve what God gives to us, but it is to say that the blessings and the provisions of God come to those who meet his conditions. When Jesus Christ died upon the cross, it didn't mean that all men everywhere would be saved. It meant that all men everywhere *could* be saved. If man meets God's conditions and commits his life to him, then everything Jesus died to bring him becomes a reality.

Here is the condition James mentions: If we are to receive the crown of life, we must love God. "And we know that all things work together for good to them that love God, to them who are the called according to his purpose" (Romans 8:28, KJV). Our lack of love for the Savior can keep God's best from coming into our lives.

In the letter to the church at Ephesus God declares, "Yet there is one thing wrong; you don't love me as at first!" (Revelation 2:4). It may be that we love God when

God does what we want him to do. It may be that we love God when he provides for us as we think he should. It may be that we try to love God on our terms. But we can't really love God like that, because the Bible says that we love him because he first loved us. His love invading our hearts and lives through our faith causes us to love him back.

Jesus came to confirm what the Old Testament revealed; namely, that the greatest commandment of all is to love God with all of our heart, mind, soul, strength, and body. If we love God with all of our heart, if today our lives are obedient to him, if we know that we have confessed every sin and have taken every step of obedience that God has sought to draw from us and our life is in the center of his will, then it can be said of us, "Blessed, happy, fortunate, prosperous are you when you endure temptation and testing because God will give to you a living crown."

5

The Root of
Temptation
James 1:13-15

"AND REMEMBER, when someone wants to do wrong it is never God who is tempting him, for God never wants to do wrong and never tempts anyone else to do it. Temptation is the pull of man's own evil thoughts and wishes. These evil thoughts lead to evil actions and afterwards to the death penalty from God" (1:13-15).

Testing and temptation are not necessarily the same thing. A trial is not necessarily an enticement to do evil. And yet we need to recognize that in every test of our faith, in every trial in our lives, in every pressure that we experience, there is an element of temptation. It contains, for example, an opportunity to become bitter or resentful, or to let animosity and hatred build. Within every trial, designed to strengthen and test our faith, there is also a temptation to evil.

In 1:13-15, James is dealing primarily with temptation to do evil. When temptation comes to us, we either overcome it or succumb to it and thus sin. Where does temptation come from? Within every man, James declares, there is a civil war. We are walking battlegrounds. Within the souls of the saved there are two natures: one that loves God and one that fights God.

Where did all this start? In Jewish thought, there were many ideas about where temptation began. Some said it started with Satan. Others felt fallen angels were responsible. Yet others believed that man himself is responsible.

Some Rabbis even put forth the idea that since God was the creator of all things, he must have created evil; he must have created in us the ability to sin.

It is out of this background that James writes this passage of Scripture, sternly rebuking any idea that God is the source of enticement to evil.

A DISTINCT REALITY

"And remember, when someone wants to do wrong..." Not "if," but "when." Every man is enticed. We cannot get away from being tempted.

What do we do when we are tempted? Where do we place the blame? Where do we find our strength? Certainly all of us would bear testimony to the reality of temptation. We all face daily temptations of anger, dishonesty, resentment, bitterness, immorality, impurity.

A DISTORTED REASONING

In man's distorted reasoning, in his mistaken judgment, he may say, "I am tempted by God." James says God "never wants to do wrong." God has no affinity toward evil. There is nothing in God that can respond to evil.

Temptation comes because we see something that we don't have that we think we need. God is perfect; he needs nothing else. He is complete within himself. There is nothing within God that needs fulfillment, satisfaction, or gratification. God is whole. His happiness is perfect. He needs nothing else.

The same perfection that makes it impossible to tempt God makes it impossible for God to tempt us. He may test us and he may allow trials to come to prove our faith, but there is nothing within God that would allow him to tempt us with evil, anymore than he himself could be tempted.

So James is saying, "God is not responsible. Don't let a man say, when he is tempted, 'I am tempted of God.' " Man has always wanted to blame someone else for his problems. In Genesis 3 we read that when God came to Adam and asked him why he did what he did, Adam said, "It was Eve's fault." Then when God went to Eve and asked her, she said, "It was the serpent's fault." We always blame others. We blame God, our fellowman, our circumstances. We say, "That is the way God made me." No, that is the way sin made us.

A DIRECT RESPONSIBILITY

"Temptation is the pull of man's own evil thoughts and wishes" (1:14). These words are fishing and hunting terms. A fish swimming along is attracted by the bait. He turns away from where he is going and takes the bait, only to discover too late that there is a hook in it. He is caught. Or there is an animal in the forest, unaware that a trap has been set in order to catch him. Something in the trap attracts his attention and he is drawn aside. When he takes the bait, he is caught.

These are the words that are used here. Every man is tempted when he is "drawn away" and "enticed" (KJV), when he is seduced or tricked. But notice where it comes from. He is drawn away by the "pull of man's own evil thoughts." The King James Version calls this "lust." The Greek word means "driving passion." It can mean passion for something good, but most of the time in the New Testament it refers to an evil passion, an uncontrollable rage or desire to get something for gain, an intense passion or consuming emotion to have something that is wrong to have.

A man is tempted and succumbs to temptation when he is attracted, seduced, enticed by his own sinfulness, his own lust. That is where sin begins—in our hearts. It is interesting that in this discussion of temptation, James never mentions Satan. One reason is that he is not giving a definitive statement about sin and its origin. He is trying to get down to the very practical working out of the truth of the Word of God. James says from a practical stand-point, "Don't blame Satan. Sin is your fault." That is really true. The temptations in our lives can be traced to our own lusts. Perhaps we give Satan too much credit. He cannot make us do anything. Whatever we do, we do because we choose to do it.

Now, lust can be for many things. It could be for power, for pleasure, for possessions, for almost anything. It is a craving, an uncontrollable passion to achieve something that we don't need. It might even be something that is legitimate, but it is such a consuming passion that it takes the wrong proportions and is pursued in the wrong ways.

How can we deal with lust? First, very simply, we must bring it to Jesus. Our desires should be in him. "Be de-lighted with the Lord. Then he will give you all your heart's desires" (Psalm 37:4). If we will give our desires to Jesus, he will put the best, the highest, and the noblest desires possible in our hearts.

Too often we allow our minds to dwell upon things that we know are not right. We allow our minds to dwell upon things of pleasure, immorality, and dishonesty, until having dwelt upon these things, our lust bursts into action and then consumes us. We need to realize that lust is nurtured by the things our eyes see, by the things our minds think about and dwell upon, by the places our feet take us, by the things our hands do, by the fellowships that we foster in our relationships. We use the members of our bodies to encourage lust. We look at the wrong things, go to the wrong places, relate to the wrong people, do the wrong things, until lust gets out of control. There is no excuse for this. "Casting down imaginations, and every high thing that exalteth itself against the knowledge of God, and bringing into captivity every thought to the obedience of Christ" (2 Corinthians 10:5, KJV). We will be controlled by our lust and desires, unless Jesus controls our lusts and desires.

Remember that there is nothing in God to respond to evil. If there were nothing within us to identify with sin, if there were no lust in our hearts to want it, no desire in our lives to achieve what we don't need or to get it in a way that is ungodly, temptation would have no appeal to us whatsoever. That is why it is important to commit our minds and hearts to Jesus Christ. If we fill our minds with lurid paperbacks or cheap television shows and movies, if we use our lips to speak words that dishonor God, if with our activities we stay away from godly people and engage in things that are not right, then we will encourage and foster lust until it becomes our master.

Some may say, "You don't understand the society that I work in." Yes, I do. I know it is difficult. But I also know that God has had through the years a core of people who trusted him and believed him and who stood victorious in the midst of the most adverse circumstances, unconquered by the evil around them. He expects that of us today!

A DELIBERATE RESULT
When all is said and done, what is the result of all this? "These evil thoughts lead to evil actions and afterwards to the death penalty from God" (1:15). The King James Version says, "when lust hath conceived, it bringeth forth

sin." "Conceive" and "bringeth forth" both speak of childbirth. James is saying, "Just as a child is a child before it is ever born from its mother, even so sin is present in the heart before it ever gives evidence that it is there." Lust in the heart conceives sin and then when sin and lust come together in opportunity, we have the inevitable result. Lust brings forth sin, and sin brings forth death.

"For the wages of sin is death . . ." (Romans 6:23a). "The soul that sinneth, it shall die" (Ezekiel 18:4, KJV). There is no exception to that. Anytime we sin, we will pay for it. Anytime we sin, we are reaping death. That doesn't mean physical death every time we sin, though physical death is the result of sin. "When Adam sinned, sin entered the entire human race. His sin spread death throughout all the world, so everything began to grow old and die" (Romans 5:12).

Whatever form sin takes, it is working against our best interest. Anytime we disobey God, we are hurting ourselves. God is not trying to make us unhappy by giving us instruction; he is trying to protect us. We must allow God to bring victory into our lives.

One thing is for sure. When we are tempted, we will never be the same again. We will either be better or we will be worse, stronger or weaker, richer or poorer, more fulfilled or more frustrated. If Hebrews 12:1, 2 means anything at all, it means that we are surrounded by a great host of witnesses—primarily God, angels, and saints who have gone on to glory. When our struggles take place, these witnesses watch with keenest interest. They know that if we withstand with God's help, we will emerge stronger and more victorious than ever before. They also know that if we fail, if we depend upon self and not God, we will become more of a slave to our own lusts.

6

The Giver of Good Gifts
James 1:16-18

"SO DON'T BE MISLED, dear brothers. But whatever is good and perfect comes to us from God, the Creator of all light, and he shines forever without change or shadow. And it was a happy day for him when he gave us our new lives, through the truth of his Word, and we became, as it were, the first children in his new family" (1:16-18).

This is a pivotal point in the chapter. James has reminded us that the problem of temptation lies in the nature of man, not in the nature of God. God may test us and God may allow us to be placed in certain situations, but he does not try to get us to sin.

When we come to verses 17 and 18, we see the flipside of the coin: any good thing, any wholesome thing originates only in God. Only good comes from God; all good originates with God. Don't be deceived into thinking there can be anything fulfilling, anything worthwhile, anything good or proper anywhere else but with God.

GOD'S INTEREST
God has a deep and abiding interest in every one of us. "Whatever is good and perfect comes to us from God, the Creator of all light." God loves to give to us. He is constantly giving us good and perfect gifts.

Let's examine "good" and "perfect." The King James Version says "good gift" and "perfect gift." In the original language there are two different words for gift. The first word speaks of the *act* of giving. Every act of giving that has good intentions, that is designed to help and to bless, is from God. The second word refers to the gift itself. James is saying, "Every act of giving that results in good and every item that is given to us that is good is from God."

The word "perfect" also means that it has no semblance of evil in it. God's gifts have nothing in them to cause us grief.

Now, an evil person may give a good gift. But whatever the secondary source, the original source of every good thing is God. Every good feeling, every good intention, every good motive that we have comes from above. What a tragic world this would be without the influence of God. We can understand how the world will be cast into great consternation and confusion during the time of great tribulation in the end of the world when the Spirit of God will no longer be at work and everything that would prompt even evil men to be kind and good will be removed from the world. Man will be left to do what he pleases, which is always evil, harmful, and hurtful to those about him.

The Greek for "comes to us" is a present participle and carries with it the wonderful meaning of continually coming. God's gifts come in a constant stream. God never stops giving to us and blessing us.

We enjoy a lot of good things. Every good relationship, every blessing—whether it be physical health, provision for our physical needs, friendships, employment, or whatever it may be—continually comes from God to us. Even the poorest of us is rich indeed because of the blessing of an eternal God upon our lives.

GOD'S IMMUTABILITY

Notice a second thing in this passage: the immutability of God. He doesn't change his basic nature. All these perfect gifts come down from the "Creator of all light, and he shines forever without change or shadow."

"Creator of all light" obviously refers to the heavenly bodies. God created all of the heavenly lights, the sun and the moon and the stars. He is the "Father of lights" (KJV). God is the very antithesis of darkness.

John said, "This is the message God has given us to pass on to you: that God is Light and in him is no darkness at all. So if we say we are his friends, but go on living in spiritual darkness and sin, we are lying. But if we are living in the light of God's presence, just as Christ does, then we have wonderful fellowship and joy with each other, and the blood of Jesus his Son cleanses us from every sin. If we say we have no sin, we are only fooling ourselves, and refusing to accept the truth. But if we confess our sins to him, he can be depended on to forgive us and to cleanse us from every wrong. (And it is perfectly proper for God to do this for us because Christ died to wash away our sins)" (1 John 1:5-9).

For one thing, this means that God is always approachable. We can always find him. Wherever the light is, he is. God does not want us to dwell in darkness, but to dwell in his light. Are we in the darkness about something? Are we confused about something? Is there an oppression in our hearts at certain points? God wants us to live in the light. It is his nature to shed the light of reason, intellect, humor, love, compassion. He longs to give understanding, purpose, and meaning to life.

Notice that James declares God is "without change." God by nature cannot change. "He shines forever without change." The sun is not as bright at dawn as it is at noonday, nor is it as bright at dusk as it is at noonday. But unlike the lights that he created, ~~God does not change.~~ We can always find God just where he said we would find him. We can always know what his response to us will be. We have access to the very heart of God, without fear of his being fickle or unpredictable.

It is wonderful to know that we have a God like that! In the midst of our sinfulness, it is good to know that we never have to question whether God still loves us. He is unchangeable in his posture toward us.

He is also "without shadow." When the sun is in eclipse, it is not the fault of the sun. The sun hasn't failed to light or shine. But something has come between the sun and the earth. It is the way the earth is turned that causes the shadow. Whenever there is a shutting off of the presence of God from our lives, it is not his failure, but ours. It is our sinfulness that has caused him to turn away. Isaiah declares that "the Lord isn't too weak to save you. And he isn't getting deaf! He can hear you when you call! But the trouble is that your sins have cut you off from God. ~~Because of sin he has turned his face away from you and will not listen anymore~~" (Isaiah 59:1, 2).

GOD'S INTENTION
"It was a happy day for him when he gave us our new lives, through the truth of his Word, and we became, as it were, the first children in his new family" (1:18).

"Gave" is a word that means "give birth to." It was the will of God to give us new birth, his greatest gift. Whatever good things we may enjoy and whatever else of significance there may be in our lives, the greatest thing that could happen is for us to know that we are saved, that Jesus Christ is in our hearts. Whether we have money, possessions, or prestige, or whatever we may seek in life, if we have been saved and born again we possess the greatest gift God could give us.

Notice: "It was a happy day for him when he gave...." God wanted us to be saved. Salvation originated in his will. It did not start out of our merit, or even out of our need, though we did need it. It started with God. Salvation, new birth, comes from God. Salvation is based on the sovereignty of God, though he requires the cooperation of man.

How is one saved? "Through the truth of his Word." The Apostle Paul says concerning Christ, "in whom ye trusted, after that ye heard the word of truth" (Ephesians 1:13, KJV). And, "for the hope which is laid up for you in heaven, whereof ye heard before in the word of the truth of the gospel" (Colossians 1:5, KJV). Peter says very simply, "being born again... by the word of God" (1 Peter 1:23, KJV). The Word of God is the instrument of salvation. Man is saved when God's Word comes alive in him. "Faith cometh by hearing, and hearing by the word of God" (Romans 10:17, KJV).

That is why the church must preach and teach the Word of God. It is not too important what we think, but it is all-important what God declares. We are born again, we are sustained, we are comforted, we are guided by the Word of truth, the Word of God.

"We became... the first children in his new family." The words "first children" mean two things. First of all, it has reference to time. We are the "first children"; there will be additional children to follow. The "firstfruits" (KJV) referred to the first harvest; there would be a later harvest as well. God did not want the gospel to stop with us. God wants us to be a vehicle through which other people may hear the Good News. God desires us to be channels through which others may be saved. A professing Christian who is not concerned about world evangelism is a contradiction. God did not save us just to make us happy, just to take us to heaven, or just to have peace in our hearts. God has given us new birth so we can help give new birth to others.

The second meaning is that the firstfruits belong totally and completely to God. They were set apart only for him. That is why in the Old Testament the people were always to give God the firstfruits; they weren't to give him the leftovers. We ought to give him the best in the flock, the best of the harvest, the best that we have. As God's firstfruits, we are God's possession. We belong to him. "Haven't you yet learned that your body is the home of the Holy Spirit God gave you, and that he lives within you? For God has bought you with a great price. So use every part of your body to give glory back to God, because he owns it" (1 Corinthians 6:19, 20).

So why do we have so many problems in our lives? It is because we don't obey him to the extent that he is able to make everything good for us. "All things work together for good to them who love God" (Romans 8:28, KJV).

The
Angry Man
James 1:19-21

"DEAR BROTHERS, don't ever forget that it is best to listen much, speak little, and not become angry; for anger doesn't make us good, as God demands that we must be. So get rid of all that is wrong in your life, both inside and outside, and humbly be glad for the wonderful message we have received, for it is able to save our souls as it takes hold of our hearts" (1:19-21).

This passage of Scripture shows us anger and what our attitude should be when we are angry. James begins by saying, "Dear brothers," a phrase of great tenderness. We are serving the same Father; we are of the same seed, the same family. It is important for us to remind ourselves of this relationship and to see in this epistle how severely James attacks those who would destroy this fellowship within the family of God.

THE ADMONITION
James says, "It is best to listen much, speak little, and not become angry." "Listen much" or "be swift to hear" (KJV) speaks of eagerness. Most of us are anxious to speak, but here we are urged to be just as quick to listen. He is talking about the Word of God, so the admonition really states,

"When you are listening to the Word of God, give careful attention. Be quick to hear what God has to say." It can be applied to other areas, but in context James is speaking primarily about the Word of God.

He goes on to say, "speak little" or be "slow to speak" (KJV). We can't listen well when we are talking. If we want to hear what God has to say, we need to listen. Prayer for us is seldom conversation; it is usually monologue. We try to tell God what we think he needs to know. But we ought to be slower to speak than to hear. The Rabbis had a saying that we have two ears and one tongue, and our tongue was put behind a wall of teeth to control it.

The Word of God has a great deal to say about hearing and speaking. "As you enter the Temple, keep your ears open and your mouth shut! Don't be a fool who doesn't even realize it is sinful to make rash promises to God, for he is in heaven and you are only here on earth, so let your words be few" (Ecclesiastes 5:1, 2). "Don't talk so much. You keep putting your foot in your mouth. Be sensible and turn off the flow!" (Proverbs 10:19). "Self-control means controlling the tongue! A quick retort can ruin everything" (Proverbs 13:3). "The man of few words and settled mind is wise; therefore, even a fool is thought to be wise when he is silent. It pays him to keep his mouth shut" (Proverbs 17:27, 28).

Now James tells us to "not become angry." It takes very little to upset us. We need to let anger become a controlled emotion. We must be slow to anger. "Angry" in the original language did not normally mean explosive anger. The anger he is talking about does not express itself outwardly, but describes an anger that sits in the heart and builds into a deep bitterness and a hostile resentment. It may express itself by grumbling to God or by complaining against our fellowman, but it is more an attitude of resistance and rebellion in the heart. Some of us never lose our

JAMES
1:19-21

temper, but we keep inside our hearts a spirit of rebellion and resentment.

"Don't be quick-tempered—that is being a fool" (Ecclesiastes 7:9). "It is better to be slow-tempered than famous; it is better to have self-control than to control an army" (Proverbs 16:32). "A short-tempered man is a fool. He hates the man who is patient (Proverbs 14:17). "A wise man controls his temper. He knows that anger causes mistakes" (Proverbs 14:29).

THE ADVERSARY

"For anger doesn't make us good, as God demands that we must be" (1:20). Man's anger does not produce the kind of goodness and righteousness God desires in us; it is our enemy. Anger that produces grumbling against God, criticism of our fellowmen, and resentment within us does not produce "the righteousness of God" (KJV). In fact, it works against it; it hinders it.

The word "anger" ("wrath," KJV) speaks of maliciousness. It is not a wrath that explodes and then is gone; it is premeditated. It is a malicious attitude, particularly toward God. The context deals with the Word of truth that we ought to be quick to hear. This anger then is an attitude of resistance to the revealed purposes of God.

This kind of anger does not produce the righteousness of God. Paul says, "Be ye angry, and sin not" (Ephesians 4:26, KJV). So God does not condemn all anger. There is a godly anger, a righteous indignation. But we must be careful because when we are angry, sin is at the door ready to come in. When things upset us and make us angry, we should ask why. Is it because it is an affront to us personally? Is it because it goes against something we want for ourselves? Then we can be sure it is the kind of anger that the devil has sponsored in our lives, and not God.

If there is an anger that comes into our lives because what we see, what we experience, what we have found at a particular point is an affront to God and we are jealous for his holiness and his righteousness, then we have righteous indignation.

What is the righteousness of God? This refers to a life that is in agreement with God, a life that is consistent with his ways, a life lived within the context of God's will and God's purpose.

THE ACTION

Now James calls us to a specific action. "So get rid of all that is wrong in your life, both inside and outside, and humbly be glad for the wonderful message we have received, for it is able to save our souls as it takes hold of our hearts" (1:21). "Get rid of" is one word in the original language, meaning to strip away, to take off. It pictures taking off that which is unnecessary for our lives or that which is contrary to God's purposes. It is a word used of a snake's shedding his skin and leaving it behind. We are to strip off that which is harmful to us.

What is harmful? "All that is wrong in your life," anything God deplores, everything evil or wicked. The King James Version calls this "filthiness." One meaning of this root word is a medical term referring to wax in the ears. Just as wax in the ears keeps one from hearing properly, so filthiness in our lives, that which is contrary to God's purpose, can keep us from hearing God properly. It can prevent God's Word from having free access into our hearts. We must put away that which will keep us from hearing the Word of truth.

Then James mentions "superfluity of naughtiness" KJV). This interesting phrase refers to what we do with each other, things we do among ourselves. The word "superfluity" is the same word used in Mark 8:8 where it says that after the 4,000 were fed, the disciples gathered up all that was left over, the overflow. The phrase here refers to exceedingly great wickedness, a wickedness so great that it not only fills up our lives, but spills over and touches those around us. We are to strip off that which is evil in our lives, because it spills over onto others. We must take away anything evil in our lives because it may cause sin in the lives of our fellow brethren.

"Humbly be glad for the wonderful message we have received, for it is able to save our souls as it takes hold of our hearts." Everything God wants to give us, he will give us only if we receive it. "To as many as *received* him, to them gave he power to become the sons of God" (John 1:12, KJV). God offers us freedom from sin, a life that is eternal both in quality and in quantity, but we must receive it. We can hear the Bible taught all of our lives, but if we don't receive it into our hearts, it will never take root and bear fruit in us.

We are to receive it "humbly." This word speaks of a teachable spirit as opposed to the arrogant spirit described earlier as the anger of man. It speaks of one who in kindness and in commitment to God has his strength and his faculties harnessed and controlled by the Spirit of God, ready to do whatever God says to do. "Meekness" (KJV) is not weakness. Rather, it is a spirit of controlled dedication.

We are to receive with a teachable spirit the "engrafted word" (KJV). "Engrafted" should be translated "implanted." It speaks of a seed that is planted and grows to produce fruit. We are to receive with hungry hearts, with teachable hearts, with a spirit of submission and love for God the implanted Word. That Word when planted in our hearts is "able to save your souls" (KJV). "Save" is the Greek word which almost always refers to ultimate salvation, salvation at the end of time. Planted in our hearts,

God's Word produces holiness of life, godliness of character, the righteousness of God.

"Get rid of" at the beginning of verse 21 is an aorist
middle participle. That simply means that the subject is
acting upon itself. It means that we are responsible for
stripping off these things. It is our responsibility to face
our need before God and commit it to him. God is not
going to barge into our lives and take these evils away
from us. He is not going to force his way into our lives and
take away that which spills over in wickedness and dis-
rupts those about us. We must come and confess our sins
to him. We must come and claim what he offers to us.

8

Living
the Word
James 1:22-25

"AND REMEMBER, it is a message to obey, not just to listen to. So don't fool yourselves. For if a person just listens and doesn't obey, he is like a man looking at his face in a mirror; as soon as he walks away, he can't see himself anymore or remember what he looks like. But if anyone keeps looking steadily into God's law for free men, he will not only remember it but he will do what it says, and God will greatly bless him in everything he does" (1:22-25).

The greatest tragedy in this century is people who gather information, but never get that information into their lives. They hear, but they never do. James is talking here about living the Word of God, about applying its truth in our lives. This is a very important passage of Scripture.

THE COMMAND

In verse 22 we notice a continuous command: "it is a message to obey" or "be ye doers" (KJV). The words "be ye" are literally "become ye" or "show yourselves to be." It is in the present tense in the original language, indicating a *kind* of action. James is declaring that we are to continuously keep on showing ourselves to be doers of the Word.

It is a sin for a believer to only occasionally rise to the mountaintop and then fall back into the valley. We are to habitually be doers of the Word. This will be underscored again at the end of this passage in verse 25.

Jesus talked about "doing the truth" (John 3:21), as did John (1 John 1:6). Truth is not information to put into our minds, but it is a life to be lived. If what we hear on Sunday does not equip us to live on Monday, we have missed the point altogether of coming to worship and we have fallen victim to this gross sin of hearing without doing.

Notice now the completion of this command. If we are not doers of the Word, James continues, we will be "hearers only" (KJV). He is not rebuking us for hearing; obviously we have to hear before we can do. The word "listen" ("hearers," KJV) was used in ancient times to describe those who came to sit and listen to lectures. Many times the word itself indicated someone who was a perpetual listener, but who never did become a disciple. They just came to listen.

There are people like that in church. They enjoy the singing, the preaching, the Bible study. They like to come and receive blessings, but they never do anything. Some people drive miles and miles to get blessed. We do not need people who want to get blessed, but people who want to be a blessing, people who want to invest their lives living the Word that they hear. It is a travesty of the Word of God to be content just to hear it. We are responsible for what we hear, responsible to incorporate it into our life, to work it out in every relationship of life.

THE CONCLUSION

A person who is content just to listen deceives and fools himself. The Bible has a great deal to say about deceiving. The word for "deceiving" (KJV) means to arrive at a conclusion by false reasoning. It would be like adding two and two and coming up with five.

If a person rejoices in the truth he hears, but does not live out that truth, he is deceiving himself. There is a great deal of difference between reading a menu and eating a meal, between holding a prescription and taking the medicine, between reading the Bible and growing in grace. We may read the Bible, come to church Sunday morning, Sunday night and Wednesday night, enjoy and be blessed by the information we receive, but we are deceiving ourselves if we think we are mature when what we have heard is not practiced in our lives.

For instance, there are some of us who often come to church, study the Word of God, have a quiet time, and yet are absolutely unbearable at home. We are unreasonable with our children and our spouses or are not the kind of workers we ought to be at work. We are lazy and do not do our jobs. Somehow we have never understood that we should do whatever we do "as unto the Lord." We should realize that everything we do reflects on Jesus. If we are not the best workers we can be, it makes Jesus look bad. If we are not kind and patient in our homes, we disgrace Jesus Christ.

We ought to hear what God has to say and then let the Holy Spirit apply that truth to our lives. We must take it home and put it into practice. We dare not be content just to listen, to go through the motions. We must do what we hear!

THE CARELESSNESS
Now James talks to us about a person who is careless with his spiritual responsibility. "For if a person just listens and doesn't obey, he is like a man looking at his face in a mirror; as soon as he walks away, he can't see himself any-

more or remember what he looks like" (1:23, 24). The word "looking" in verse 23 is a very descriptive word. It refers to a casual, haphazard approach to looking at something, a glance. Many people see, but they don't see. They look at something, but they don't really see anything. Or they see what they want, but they don't see what is really there. If we hear the Word but don't do it, we are like the person who carelessly looks into a mirror and then forgets what he sees.

A careless person makes mistakes. If a man is careless on an assembly line where he does nothing but put a piece of metal beneath a punch, he is likely to lose his hand underneath the machine someday. He cannot afford to be casual or careless. We dare not treat the Word of God casually either.

Before you last went to worship, did you ask God to prepare your heart to receive what his Word had for you? Did you thank God for what he was going to show you? Or did you just go to church because it was Sunday? That is approaching the Word of God carelessly.

"As soon as he walks away, he can't see himself anymore or remember what he looks like." This pictures a person who looks and then walks away unaffected by what he has seen. He is not even aware that it makes any difference. That is why a person can go to church, hear the Word, sing and pray, and then go out and lie and steal. He never took to heart what he heard. He hears but does not act. He forgets what manner of man he was; he forgets what he has seen.

When we look into the Word of God, we see ourselves for what we are. The word "face" in verse 23 literally means the face nature gave us, ourselves as we really are. The man who looks into the Word of God sees that the "heart is deceitful and desperately wicked" and that "all have sinned and come short of the glory of God." He sees that "all have turned everyone to his own way" and rebelled against God. He sees himself, but it doesn't affect his life at all. He rationalizes, thinking no one will know or that his sin will not affect too many people very seriously. He does not view the sin in his life as an affront to the holiness of God who has created him. He views sin in a flippant, casual, careless way and forgets what he saw. What a tragedy it is when we don't apply what God's Word reveals to us.

Sadly, there are millions of professing Christians whose lives are so unaffected by the Word of God that those who work with them do not even know if they are saved. If we know the Lord, it ought to make a difference in the way we treat our families, how we work at our jobs, how we relate to our friends, how we file our income tax returns, how we drive our automobiles. It ought to make a difference in our lives. But a person who just carelessly glances into the mirror of the Word of God will go on his way unaffected by it. He will not live the truth he has heard.

THE COMMITMENT

Verse 25 is really the heart of what James is saying to us. "But if anyone keeps looking steadily into God's law for free men, he will not only remember it but he will do what it says, and God will greatly bless him in everything he does" (1:25). The conjunction "but" tells us that James is going to talk now about the man who doesn't treat the Word of God casually.

The word "looking" in verse 23 speaks of casualness, but "looking" in verse 25 speaks of commitment. When the disciples ran to the tomb of Jesus and found that he was risen from the dead, "they stooped and looked in" (Luke 24:12; John 20:5). They found the tomb empty, the stone rolled away. And the grave clothes were there. They "looked" about and studied every detail; they saw the evidence of the resurrected Christ. The word that is translated "stooped" is identical with this word "looking" in verse 25. It means to carefully, intently study something, to look at it with the full attention of our hearts and souls, to give it our undivided attention.

When we come to the Word of God, there should be diligent pursuit of its truth. It ought to be something we give our best attention to. We shouldn't miss any details, but see everything that is before us. We must study it carefully and let it be applied in our lives.

James calls it "the perfect law of liberty" (KJV). The Greek language literally says, "a perfect law, the liberty." The law is perfect and it results in liberty. It is a perfect law because God gave it to us, and whatever God gives is perfect.

Furthermore, the man who hears it and applies it, allowing the Holy Spirit to put it into his life, will himself become perfect, complete, and whole. "Perfect" in the New Testament means full-grown, mature. As we apply that law and let it work itself into our lives, we will become what God wants us to be.

"A perfect law of liberty" sounds like a paradox. If we are under law, we are required to do a certain thing and that is not liberty. If I am under the law of the state of Texas, I am not at liberty to drive on the highways at 70 miles an hour when the limit is 55 miles an hour. How can there be such a thing as a law of liberty?

Very simply, God gives us a law that is the strictest law we could possibly have. The Christian law that is placed upon us is far more strict than the Old Testament law. It is far more strict than any pagan law or any law of human government. It is a law that requires every thought to be brought into captivity. It is a law that requires us to love God with our hearts, souls, and minds, everything that we are. It is a law that says, "All that you are, all that you possess belongs to God." It is a binding, heavy law that God places upon us. How then is it the law of liberty? Because the God who requires so much of us works in our hearts to produce exactly what he requires!

He tells us to love him, and then he works in our lives in such a gracious way that we do love him. He tells us that we are to live a certain way, and then he works in our lives in such a way that we want to live the way he wants us to live. The law tells us that we are to hate sin, but then God works in us to reveal his grace and love toward us so that we do hate sin. He produces in us that which he requires of us.

He teaches me that I am to pray. But when I pray, I find it is what my heart longs to do. I love praying because he has changed my life. He tells a mother to love her children. And, unless you are an unusual mother, you love loving your children. What God requires of us is what our hearts delight in doing. Isn't that amazing? If our heart does not delight in obeying God, in living for him and doing his Word, then we need to come back to this basic commitment and be sure that our lives are yielded to God, that our sins are confessed, and that we have allowed him to work in us because his law is a law of liberty. It requires everything that we are, but it gives to us the desire and the ability to do what is required.

The Bible requires us to faithfully participate in the worship of the family of God. And those of us who come find that though it is required, we love being together. What God requires of us, he puts in our heart to do. What we need to do, we long to do. What we are asked to do, we love doing. In obeying the law, we are set free.

If there is any point of disobedience in our lives, we are bound. If there is anything we know God wants us to do and we haven't done it, we are bound by the law. But if we will do what God commands us to do, we will find in doing it that we are set free and we love doing it. We find fulfillment in doing what God has required us to do.

The beautiful thing about this law is that it is a law that not only results in liberty or freedom, but it is also a law that we voluntarily respond to. We have to choose to do it. God will not make us do it. We have to bow our knees to him, commit our lives to him.

After talking about commitment, James speaks of necessary discipline. "But if anyone keeps looking steadily into God's law for free men. . . ." This matter of being a Christian is not a haphazard experience. Christianity is a life to be lived. The words "keep looking steadily" mean "to remain." If we remain in the Word of God, if we continue faithful to it, if we continue hearing it, applying it, and living it, then God can bless us in a great way. If our discipline keeps us in it, we won't be forgetful hearers, but doers of the Word. "This man" (KJV) is in the emphatic position in the original language, meaning "this man alone." "This man shall be blessed in his deed." The idea is that he is blessed while he is doing it. As we apply the Word of God and do what he has told us to do, we will be blessed in the doing of it.

"God's laws are pure, eternal, just. They are more desirable than gold. They are sweeter than honey dripping from a honeycomb. For they warn us away from harm and give success to those who obey them" (Psalm 19:9-11). "Blessed are they that keep judgment, and he that doeth righteousness at all times (Psalm 106:3, KJV). "Happy are all who search for God, and always do his will" (Psalm 119:2). "Blessed is he that keepeth the sayings of the prophecy of this book" (Revelation 22:7, KJV). "You know these things—now do them! That is the path of blessing" (John 13:17).

In Luke we read about a woman who came praising Jesus and he rebuked her. It is easier to say "Amen" and shout "Hallelujah" than to do what we ought to do. There are many people who go around praising God but live like the devil. That is what this woman was apparently doing. Jesus said, "Yes, but even more blessed are all who hear the Word of God and put it into practice" (Luke 11:28).

James is reminding us of the great tragedy that takes place thousands of times every Sunday, every Wednesday, every time there is a Bible study across this land or around the world where people come and hear the Word of God, listen to it, but do not do anything about it. They are no different than when they came. There is no change in their lives. There is no application of truth to their experience.

Worship is not complete until we have had an encounter with God. As we act upon that which the Holy Spirit has prompted us to do, we will find that life will be blessed, and that which we are required to do, we will love doing. God forbid that we should simply listen and not hear; observe and not see; think and not know. Rather, may we become doers of the Word by our personal commitment and obedience.

Genuine
Religion
James 1:26, 27

9

"ANYONE WHO SAYS he is a Christian but doesn't control his sharp tongue is just fooling himself, and his religion isn't worth much. The Christian who is pure and without fault, from God the Father's point of view, is the one who takes care of orphans and widows, and who remains true to the Lord—not soiled and dirtied by his contacts with the world" (1:26, 27).

These important verses describe the essence of real and pure religion. James has already talked about being doers of the Word, and now he gives us some illustrations of how to be doers of the Word.

Verse 26 talks about false worship, and verse 27 talks to us about true worship. Worship is the essence of religion; if a man does not truly worship God, he has no genuine religion.

FALSE RELIGION

First of all, false religion has a lack of reality to it. There is something phony about it. "Anyone who says . . ." "If any man among you seem to be religious . . ." (KJV). The word "says" or "seem" means to appear according to one's own estimate. Here is a man who thinks he is a religious person, a spiritual person, and yet he "is just fooling himself."

The person who has a false religion is simply repeating words that belong to someone else. For years and years I tried to preach on the Lordship of Christ, and I couldn't do it, until one day I experienced the Lordship of Christ in my life. Since then, it has been a joy to preach about it. Now it is part of me.

False religion is always insecure and unreal, because a man seems to be something that he is not. We are not talking about the hypocrite, the man who puts on a front, knowing in his heart that he is a reprobate. Here we are talking about a person who sincerely thinks that he is serving God, and yet there is something unreal about his profession. James has already said a man who hears the Word and doesn't put it into action does not have the right kind of faith. False religion occurs when a man says all the right words, talks the language, has fooled himself into thinking he is something he is not, but his religion is false and worthless.

Secondly, this verse tells us that false religion has a lack of restraint to it—". . . doesn't control his tongue . . ." The original language literally says that we are to keep our tongues in our cheeks. Some people think they prove their spirituality by the wisdom with which they discuss theological matters. But James is saying that one of the real tests of spirituality is when we know how to keep quiet.

Satan can use the tongue to destroy lives. With a word a heart is lifted or cast down. With a word our spirits are dashed or they are encouraged. With a word there is sweetness or bitterness. With a word there is victory or defeat. False religion is characterized by a loose tongue. We are to bridle the tongue.

"Anyone who says he is a Christian but doesn't control his sharp tongue is just fooling himself." If we find ourselves always being critical and condemning, if that is the

first thing that comes to our minds, if we are always
finding something to be unhappy about, then we have
deceived ourselves and do not have the religion of the
New Testament. No real faith produces that kind of action.

Also, false religion lacks results—"his religion isn't
worth much." "Religion" in this verse is the word which
refers to the outward expression of formal religion. It
means going through the motions of worship, the ritual,
the liturgy, the singing, the praying. It is not the word for
a deep love for God and the deep worship of our hearts.
It depicts outward religion. False religion looks religious
only when it is at religious meetings. When it is some-
where else, it is something else. True Christianity is more
than going to church. It is more than a way of doing certain
things such as singing, praying, or witnessing. Christianity is a certain way of doing everything.

God says false religion is "vain" (KJV); i.e., futile,
worthless, fruitless, of no value whatsoever. Listen to
what God said to the people of Israel through his prophet
Isaiah: "I am sick of your sacrifices. Don't bring me any
more of them. I don't want your fat rams; I don't want to
see the blood from your offerings. Who wants your
sacrifices when you have no sorrow for your sins? The
incense you bring me is a stench in my nostrils" (Isaiah
1:11, 12). They were coming without adequate preparation. They were trampling underfoot the dignity and the
reverence of the worship of God. So he said, "I want
nothing more to do with them. I hate them all; I can't
stand the sight of them. From now on, when you pray
with your hands stretched out to heaven, I won't look or
listen. Even though you make many prayers, I will not
hear, for your hands are those of murderers; they are
covered with the blood of your innocent victims. Oh,
wash yourselves! Be clean! Let me no longer see you doing
all these wicked things; quit your evil ways. Learn to do
good, to be fair and to help the poor, the fatherless, and

widows. Come, let's talk this over! says the Lord; no matter how deep the stain of your sins, I can take it out and make you as clean as freshly fallen snow. Even if you are stained as red as crimson, I can make you white as wool!" (Isaiah 1:13-18).

That last verse is often applied to the lost. In reality, it is a verse that was given to his people who had come in a false way to obey his laws. We can sin by coming to church. We sin by going through the motions of religion without our hearts being committed to God as they ought to be.

TRUE RELIGION

Verse 27 pictures true religion. Notice that true worship is "pure and without fault, from God the Father's point of view." If we would be as concerned about how we look before God when we come into his house as we are about how we look to each other, it would make a great deal of difference. If we would spend the time in spiritual preparation that we spend in physical preparation, we would be much stronger.

Notice the two illustrations of pure religion: "one who takes care of orphans and widows and who remains true to the Lord—not soiled and dirtied by his contacts with the world."

First, he says, "takes care of orphans and widows." Some people will read a verse like this and conclude that all we have to do is visit the fatherless and the widows and keep unspotted from the world and that is all God requires. That is not what James is saying. He declares that our lives will express themselves in certain ways as we have real love for God and a genuine commitment to him. It must begin in the heart.

The words "takes care" come from the Greek word

from which we get our title "bishop" or "overseer." The word does not indicate a casual visit, but deep spiritual concern. We are to oversee them. We are to love them. We are to care for them. We are to provide for them. We are to get involved in their needs and their lives.

In that day as in this day, the fatherless and the widows were especially vulnerable to evil and to exploitation. In that day especially, the fatherless were vagabonds of the streets, often victims of slavetraders and other abuse. And widows had no particular standing at all. Many of them of necessity turned to immorality and the ways of the world in order to sustain themselves. So James is saying that we should shield them and protect them. We will serve God as we serve them.

Whose life are we touching for God? Whom are we helping with their needs, physical as well as spiritual? Real worship is going to result in such an overseeing and care for the fatherless and the widows.

The word "affliction" (KJV) is translated elsewhere "burden," "anguished," "troubled," "persecution," "tribulation." It pictures someone who is under pressure, someone who has stumbled and faces a crisis in their lives or their home. We can see that all around us today. James reminds us that real religion is going to take us out where the pressure is, where people's difficulties are, touching lives where people hurt and where they desperately need us. That is real religion.

True religion, he continues, is to "remain true to the Lord—not soiled and dirtied by his contacts with the world." It is no coincidence that he put this statement immediately after urging us to care for orphans and widows. The best way for us to quit being worldly, to avoid temptation, to keep ourselves unspotted from the world is to be involved in serving God by ministering to other people. As we give ourselves to service, to being involved in the lives of other people, we are kept pure and clean from the world.

This matter of being pure and clean from the world indicates to us that we are not of the world. The Christian can never be at home here. Does that mean that we cannot enjoy our work or our families? Not at all! The idea of "the world" means the evil of the world; the child of God will never be at home with evil men. If we find ourselves comfortable with things of the world, with immorality, with vulgarity and profanity, with dishonesty and lying, with criticism and gossip, then we are not God's children. Real religion means we are kept "unspotted" from the world. We do not find our joy or peace in it.

Our joy is in the Lord. We are to invest ourselves in that which is eternal, in the things of God.

As we serve God, we find an effective shield from the world. God wants us to be busy. Idleness is the devil's workshop in our lives. It was while King David was loafing on the roof of his palace, rather than leading his troops into battle, that he fell into immorality with Bathsheba. When we are not busy serving God, Satan will destroy us. But as we busily serve God, we will keep ourselves unspotted from the world.

10

The Period
of Patronage
James 2:1-9

"DEAR BROTHERS, how can you claim that you belong to the Lord Jesus Christ, the Lord of glory, if you show favoritism to rich people and look down on poor people? If a man comes into your church dressed in expensive clothes and with valuable gold rings on his fingers, and at the same moment another man comes in who is poor and dressed in threadbare clothes, and you make a lot of fuss over the rich man and give him the best seat in the house and say to the poor man, 'You can stand over there if you like, or else sit on the floor'—well, judging a man by his wealth shows that you are guided by wrong motives.

"Listen to me, dear brothers: God has chosen poor people to be rich in faith, and the Kingdom of Heaven is theirs, for that is the gift God has promised to all those who love him. And yet, of the two strangers, you have despised the poor man. Don't you realize that it is usually the rich men who pick on you and drag you into court? And all too often they are the ones who laugh at Jesus Christ, whose noble name you bear. Yes indeed, it is good when you truly obey our Lord's command, 'You must love and help your neighbors just as much as you love and take care of yourself.' But you are breaking this law of our Lord's when you favor the rich and fawn over them; it is sin" (2:1-9).

This passage deals with the problem of partiality, with the problem of patronizing those who seem to have characteristics or qualities that we like more than others. It is a problem that existed in the early church, and we are still experiencing the same problem although nearly 2,000 years have passed.

THE COMMAND

In the first four verses James illustrates the fact that more preference is given to a man who has wealth, while dishonor is given to one who doesn't have such prestige and riches.

In verse 1, James tells us not to show "favoritism." There ought to be no snobbery in the church. Wherever God's people gather, there should be no distinction between them.

In the early church, a man with many slaves might come into a worship service and find the service being presided over by his slaves. We can see how that might pose some problems. The social distinctions of that day would have been a very difficult thing to combat. But James is saying that whenever God's people gather, we gather as equals. Each member of the body of Christ is as important as the other. The needs of one are just as vital as the needs of another. Social snobbery is an enemy of the fellowship of the church.

James is striking here the same note that he has declared all the way along: our creed and conduct ought to be the same. What we say we believe and what we do ought to be consistent. We should not claim to be Christians if we don't live like Christians.

Who is "the Lord of glory"? Most scholars believe this is a title for Jesus. In John 17, Jesus begins praying by saying, "Father, the hour is come; glorify thy Son, that thy Son may also glorify thee: . . . I have glorified thee on the earth; I have finished the work which thou gavest me to do. And now, O Father, glorify thou me with thine own self with the glory which I had with thee before the world was" (John 17:1, 4, 5, KJV).

We violate our Christian profession by showing favoritism. The words translated "respect of persons" (KJV) indicate that there are many ways we can do this, though James reminds us of only one of the ways by the example of the church service itself.

The words mean "to lay hold of one's face"; i.e., "lay hold of what one appears to be." We see the mask that someone wears, whether it is a mask of wealth, dignity, or culture, and lay hold on what we see. We make a judgment based upon what we see when the person enters the church.

James gives the illustration of a rich man and a poor man, both evidently visitors. It seems that they both wanted flattery. Some say that the poor man wanted charity. The rich man wanted flattery. In this case, the poor is denied help and the rich is given praise. Perhaps flattery is given because the man is wealthy and can do some good.

One of the great dangers of the church is to look for people who can help us instead of looking for people we can help. Too many Christians want to be blessed instead of being a blessing. Some churches seem to build their fellowship out of those who can contribute something rather than finding those who need help.

The word for "church" referred both to the Jewish assembly as well as the Christian assembly. Back then the front seats were the seats of honor. So they ushered the rich man to the seat of honor and told the poor man he could stand in the back or sit on the floor. They made a judgment that was in direct contradiction to what Jesus Christ told them should be their attitude. Their judgment was guided by "wrong motives." That phrase means to judge with evil intentions.

THE CHOICE

Verse 5 uses the phrase, "my beloved brethren" (KJV). James started off calling them "my brethren"; now he calls them "my beloved brethren." The angrier he gets at them, the more he has to love them. This is a good lesson for us. If we are going to reprimand, we need to do it in love. James is not really angry with them; he is angry with the sin that has perverted them. He loved them, but despised the conduct that he described.

"God has chosen poor people." It was in the sovereignty of God that the Christian gospel was embraced by the poor. One of the greatest dangers the church has today is not its poverty, but its prosperity, its affluence. Affluence and spirituality don't seem to mix. And it was so then. It was not that the early church did not minister to the wealthy, but wealthy people had a difficult time coming to Jesus.

God chose the poor. In fact, God chooses all his people. "Ye have not chosen me, but I have chosen you" (John 15:16, KJV). "God hath from the beginning chosen you to salvation through sanctification of the Spirit and belief of the truth" (2 Thessalonians 2:13b, KJV). "But ye are a chosen generation, a royal priesthood, an holy nation, a peculiar people" (1 Peter 2:9, KJV). No man is saved until God calls him to be saved, until God reaches out, convicts, and draws him to salvation.

James says, "God made a choice and he chose the poor. And yet you chose just the opposite. God chose the poor, but you chose the rich." It is amazing how God's judgment and man's judgment are so often opposite.

"And yet . . . you have despised the poor man." "Despised" means "dishonored." That which God chose, they dishonored.

"It is usually the rich men who pick on you and drag you into court." The rich used their power and position against Christians. We see this in the book of Acts. Saul of Tarsus used legal action from the Sanhedrin to capture and put to death Christians.

"And all too often they are the ones who laugh at Jesus Christ, whose noble name you bear" (2:7). These Christians gave deference to the very people who were their enemies in the faith, who wanted to destroy what they stood for.

We need to stand firm on our convictions. There is so much compromise in the fellowship of churches today simply because someone has some prestige, power, or money. It is amazing how much we condone in people we want to get something from. The church that pleases God is one that will not compromise its convictions, will not stop standing upon the solid rock of the Word of God and the revelation of Jesus Christ, but will insist on purity and compassion and holiness on the part of its members.

They "laugh at Jesus Christ, whose noble name you bear." The book of Acts tells us that the name Christian was given first in ridicule at Antioch. It was a term of derision. Men love to ridicule and blaspheme the name of Jesus Christ.

Many people today use the name of Jesus Christ in profanity. Why don't they ever get mad and say "Jimmy Carter!" or "Socrates!" Why do they profane the name of Jesus Christ? Because it is the nature of those who do not know God to blaspheme him.

There are several meanings of the phrase "whose noble name you bear." The King James Version translates it, "that worthy name by which you are called." One of the meanings is, "the name by which God claimed you." We belong to him. He has claimed us and has given us his name. The word "called" is used in the Bible to refer to a wife taking her husband's name, and also of a son taking his father's name. We are called Christian; we are called sons of God.

THE CONDEMNATION

"Yes indeed, it is good when you truly obey our Lord's command, 'You must love and help your neighbors just as much as you love and take care of yourself' " (2:8). We can almost hear some of the Christians objecting, "We have only been doing what God told us to do. He told us to love our neighbor as ourselves." So James says, almost with tongue in cheek, "If that is really why you are giving such deference to the rich man, then you do well. But if you have respect to persons, if it is just an excuse, you are committing a sin and are breaking God's law."

James calls God's law the "royal law" (2:8, KJV). It may be the royal law because of its source—God. He is King of kings and Lord of lords. It could be a royal law because of the high standards of that law.

Without question, love is the law that God wants us to live by. Our love for each other, a love that keeps our hearts bound together, a love that gives fellowship and encouragement to each other is God's ideal. But if we have respect of persons, we are "breaking this law." "Breaking" could be translated "convicted." We have been tried and convicted of the law as transgressors.

Most of our sins are "respectable" sins. Few people know about them. Not very many people know what is in our hearts. But God does. If we honor one person and put down another, he will deal with us.

"God has chosen poor people to be rich in faith" (2:5). Their richness lies in their faith. When we live by faith, we are wealthy. We have all that we need. All that is God's is ours as we walk in his presence, live in his power, and claim the promises he has given to us.

So, don't look at the masks or the circumstances. We must love and honor others for what they are, not for what we think they are. Don't be partial to some, but in a relationship of love serve God together, obey God together, worship together so that we will all be shielded and protected.

11
The Law
of Liberty
James 2:10-13

WHAT DOES IT MEAN to violate the law of God? James now elaborates on this important question.

THE CONDEMNATION

"And the person who keeps every law of God, but makes one little slip, is just as guilty as the person who has broken every law there is. For the God who said you must not marry a woman who already has a husband, also said you must not murder, so even though you have not broken the marriage laws by committing adultery, but have murdered someone, you have entirely broken God's laws and stand utterly guilty before him" (2:10, 11).

It is important that we understand this truth because we have done very much like the Jews. The ancient Jew looked at the law of God as a disjointed group of injunctions, considering some to be of more importance than others. Their attitude toward the law ignored great portions of it and meticulously kept other parts. They believed that if they kept as many laws as they broke, they were righteous before the law.

James is putting a knife to the very heart of this attitude. He is very clearly declaring that if we even offend on one point, we are as guilty as one who has broken every law. In context, James is talking specifically about being disrespectful to some people while giving honor to others. And he is dealing with the habitual practice of it. In verse 9, the words translated "favor the rich and fawn over them" is in the present tense, indicating continuous action. He has just accused them of having an habitual attitude of partiality and told them that it is a sin. Now he tells them that if they keep the whole law, and yet habitually offend at one point, they are transgressors of the whole law.

He is not talking about just an isolated act, but about making rebellion against God a pattern of life, yet passing over it because we keep the rest of the law.

If the practice of our lives is to flout God's will and God's purposes, even on one point, God declares we are guilty of all. We cannot pick and choose what we will obey in God's law. We all want to do that. There are some sins that are no problem to us; but there are other sins we enjoy. But we can't pick and choose. All sins are equally evil.

People often say, "I have never killed anyone. I am not a thief. I am not immoral." But they have lied or neglected the Word of God or failed to speak up for Christ or done some other sin. We are all guilty.

James is not saying that one sin is as bad as another. He is not saying that it would be just as bad for us to be disrespectful to someone as it would be for us to kill someone. He is not talking about the degree of guilt, but is simply saying that there is real guilt if we violate the law at any point. Not every link in a chain has to be broken for a chain to be broken.

Within our prison system are many kinds of criminals. One man may be a murderer. Another is guilty of perjury. But both of them are viewed as criminals. James is not comparing the two, but is simply saying that a man who breaks any of the law is guilty in God's sight.

There are a thousand doors to rebellion, many of them secret. For every man whose violations of the laws of God are made public, there are thousands of us who transgress secretly. Perhaps we fall to jealousy, pride, self-righteousness, or lust. However we disobey God, we are sinners.

James calls God's law "the law of liberty" (2:12, KJV) because it frees us to enjoy the greatest fulfillment we could possibly know. It is a law that we obey, not because of fear of punishment or because we are coerced into it, but because God plants his love in our lives. This love causes us to want to obey the law.

THE CONDUCT
"You will be judged on whether or not you are doing what Christ wants you to. So watch what you do and what you think; for there will be no mercy to those who have shown no mercy. But if you have been merciful, then God's mercy toward you will win out over his judgment against you" (2:12, 13). In light of the fact that we are accountable to God and will someday stand in judgment before him, our lives ought to manifest our commitment to him in Christian love. Earlier James declared, "Yes indeed, it is good when you truly obey our Lord's command, 'You must love and help your neighbors just as much as you love and take care of yourself' " (2:8). If we loved our neighbors as we love ourselves, it would free us from self-righteousness, condemnation, criticism, jealousy, lust, envy.

"You will be judged on whether or not you are doing what Christ wants you to. So watch what you do and what you think" (2:12). If we live our lives in the awareness of judgment, it will make a difference. "Young man, it's wonderful to be young! Enjoy every minute of it! Do all you want to; take in everything, but realize that you must account to God for everything you do" (Ecclesiastes 11:9). "Here is my final conclusion: fear God and obey his commandments, for this is the entire duty of man. For God will judge us for everything we do, including every hidden thing, good or bad" (Ecclesiastes 12:13, 14). "Yes, each of us will give an account of himself to God" (Romans 14:12).

James then goes on to say we will be judged by the same standards with which we judge. We must be careful here, lest we think that if we show mercy and compassion, then we will receive mercy and compassion. That would be a salvation by works.

James is simply saying that if we have been saved by the grace of God, then his grace will make us gracious. The gracious spirit in us is evidence that we have been touched by God's grace. If we have received the mercy of God, we then will demonstrate mercy; his mercy in us will produce mercy toward others. Our conduct is a direct correlation to our relationship to God. If we find it in our hearts to always be critical and condemning, that reveals a deficient relationship with God. If we find it in our hearts always to be overbearing and feel superior to other people, passing judgment upon them, it is evidence of a lack of a real relationship with God. The judgments that come from us ought to be produced by God's Spirit within us. Our conduct is a demonstration of our relationship with God.

What is "the law of liberty" (2:12, KJV)? It was called "the royal law" (KJV) in verse 8. That law tells us to love our neighbor as ourselves. We obey God's laws because we love God. We are gracious to God's people because we love God's people. We are under a law of love.

One of the most significant revelations of the Christian faith is this: "This is the agreement I will make with the people of Israel, though they broke their first agreement: I will write my laws into their minds so that they will always know my will, and I will put my laws in their hearts so that they will want to obey them." And then he adds, "I will never again remember their sins and lawless deeds" (Hebrews 10:16, 17). The Old Testament Jew obeyed the law of God though he didn't understand it. But now God is writing his law in our minds. He has given to us his Word as a revelation of his purpose and will.

Many times the ancient Jew did what God told him to do because he was afraid not to. We obey because we love God. Because of his work in our hearts, we love doing his law. If we know Jesus Christ and walk in a relationship with him, we will love him. To disobey him would break our hearts. If we find it easy to sin, to carry wrong attitudes and to conduct a spirit of arrogance towards others, then there is something terribly wrong. If God's love is in our hearts, we will love doing his will.

THE COMPASSION

"For there will be no mercy to those who have shown no mercy. But if you have been merciful, then God's mercy toward you will win out over his judgment against you" (2:13). If our lives have been characterized by overbearing condemnation of others, if we have condemned others because of their failure, it will be evident that we have not received the mercy of God and we will not receive mercy. Judgment without mercy will be given to the man who has shown no mercy.

We don't want justice, but mercy when we come before God. If we have not received his mercy, then we will be condemned forever. But if we have received his mercy, then we will stand before God without condemnation. We will not be judged guity because his mercy covers us.

"So there is now no condemnation awaiting those who belong to Christ Jesus. For the power of the life-giving Spirit—and this power is mine through Christ Jesus—has freed me from the vicious circle of sin and death" (Romans 8:1, 2). We are guilty before God; our only hope is God's mercy.

Remember, James is not a theologian. This is a book of practical Christianity. James is simply saying that if we have received the mercy of God, we will be merciful persons.

Does that mean that we can wink at sin? Not at all! We should denounce sin, but not the sinner. Jesus loved the sinner, though he despised the sin that destroyed him. Jesus died upon the cross, bearing our sins because he loved us as individuals. That is how important we are to God. That is how much God loves us.

If we were God, there are some folks we would enjoy punishing. That shows an area of our lives in which God needs to do some work. Whenever we see weaknesses in each other, we ought to weep with a broken heart because their sin is an affront to God. Though we despise what they do, we should love them and care about them.

The law of God is less concerned about forbidding certain sins than it is about admonishing us to have certain virtues which make those sins impossible. God would rather give us something positive to do than something negative not to do.

Let's use an illustration from these thirteen verses. Rather than saying to us, "You are not to bear false witness against your neighbor," God said, "You are to love your neighbor as yourself." Just because we don't say something bad about our neighbor doesn't mean we have fulfilled the law. We haven't fulfilled the law unless we love him. And if we love him, we will be very slow to believe anything bad about him and even less in a hurry to say anything bad about him.

It is not enough to not retaliate against our enemies. We ought to so love them that retaliation is impossible. God's law in us doesn't just say, "Don't lie. Don't cheat.

Don't steal. Don't commit adultery. Don't kill." It says, "Love God with all of your heart and mind and soul." If we love God like that, and if we love our neighbors as ourselves, we won't blaspheme God, because we love him. We won't commit immorality because it is a sin against ourselves and God. We will not steal because it is an assault upon the integrity of God. We would not infringe on the rights of others because we love them and God. Love fulfills the law.

Whatever God asks us to do, we ought to do it. The love that God plants in our lives will express itself in what we say and what we do.

WHEN WE COME to these verses, we are confronted with
one of the most misunderstood and certainly one of the
most controversial passages of Scripture anywhere in the
Word of God. There are those who have said that James
preaches a doctrine of salvation by works, the Apostle
Paul preaches a doctrine of salvation by faith through
grace, and there is a conflict between them. They point to
this passage of Scripture as evidence of that supposed dis-
crepancy. However, we will discover that this is not the
case. The two New Testament authors were not declaring
opposing views of salvation, but were discussing two
different kinds of faith. James deals here with genuine
faith and counterfeit faith.

We need to understand that James and Paul preach out
of different circumstances. Paul was combatting those
who said that salvation came by keeping the works of the
Mosaic law. James was talking about the antinomians who
said, "I am saved, so I can live any way I want." He was
refuting a heresy claiming that salvation has no bearing on
how we live.

James and Paul used words in different contexts and
with different connotations. When Paul talks about
"works," he is speaking about the works of the Jewish

law, such as circumcision and sacrifices. When James speaks of works, he is talking about works of love, obedience, kindness, graciousness—i.e., our obedience to God based upon our love for God.

When the Apostle Paul speaks of the word "justified," he is talking about the initial experience of salvation whereby a man is declared righteous before God and acquitted of his sins. He reaches this redemption by faith. When James uses the word "justified," he is using it in the sense of vindication. James says our faith is proved by our works. We need to understand that James is not talking about how a person is saved. Primarily he is speaking about those who say they are saved but are not. If we say one thing and live another, we prove ourselves to be untrue.

THE CLAIM

"Dear brothers, what's the use of saying that you have faith and are Christians if you aren't proving it by helping others? Will *that* kind of faith save anyone?" (2:14). The key in this passage is the word "saying." Notice that he is not stating, "if a man has faith," but "if a man *says* he has faith." But faith cannot be seen. How do we know we have faith? James says a faith that is not seen, proven, evidenced by behavior is not faith at all. Can that kind of faith save? In the original Greek, there is the definite article "that" before faith—can "that kind of faith" save? This rhetorical question can only be answered in the negative. A man who claims to have faith and yet his life is barren of any evidence of faith is lying. That kind of faith can never bring salvation.

Then James gives an illustration: If someone comes along who is naked and destitute of daily food and we pat him on the back, tell him we will pray for him, and don't provide for his needs, we have not done him any good. That kind of encouragement doesn't help him or us. Here is someone who has the means to help the hungry or one who needs clothing, but instead he only offers verbal encouragement. That kind of faith is of no profit at all. "What good does that do?" (2:16).

A person who claims to have faith but whose life doesn't show it has faith that is "dead and useless" (2:17). "Dead" means barren, useless, without any value. Throughout this book, James says if we are saved, we will show our salvation by the way we live. A man who says he has faith but does not live it does not have saving faith.

That is not uniquely a doctrine of James. The Apostle Paul teaches us the same thing. "When someone becomes a Christian he becomes a brand new person inside. He is not the same any more. A new life has begun!" (2 Corinthians 5:17). That is the teaching throughout the New Testament. If a man is in Christ, his life has been transformed. In a passage often quoted as being in conflict with this passage, Paul says, "For by grace are ye saved through faith; and that not of yourselves: it is the gift of God: not of works, lest any man should boast" (Ephesians 2:8, 9, KJV). Immediately he goes on to say "For we are his workmanship, created in Christ Jesus unto good works, which God hath before ordained that we should walk in them." We are not saved by works; but if we are saved, we will walk in the path that God has ordained we should walk. James is not saying that any man with works is saved, but that any man without works is not saved. If our lives do not reflect the presence of God in the way we live, we have not met Jesus Christ.

That does not mean that a Christian will never sin, but it means that a person who habitually lives in sin away from God has a counterfeit faith. We need to be careful that we do not claim something that is not ours.

THE CREED

Concerning these people who say they have faith, James says, "Are there still some among you who hold that 'only believing' is enough? Believing in one God? Well, remember that the demons believe this too—so strongly that they tremble in terror! Fool! When will you ever learn that 'believing' is useless without *doing* what God wants you to? Faith that does not result in good deeds is not real faith" (2:19, 20). There are many people who believe the right things. They believe that Jesus is the Son of God, that he died for our sins, that he is coming again. The devil believes all that too; that is why he trembles. "Tremble" is an interesting word. It means "to bristle." It pictures one's hair standing up on end. The devil believes in God so strongly that his hair stands right up on end! But he is still the enemy of God. We can believe all the right words and say the right creed, but that doesn't save us. There are a lot of Bible-toting folks who will go to hell.

Belief is something we do. The Apostle John talks about "doing" the truth (John 3:21; 1 John 1:6). If what we believe is simply a creed, if we only profess to believe certain facts intellectually, then we are not even doing as much as the demons, because they believe and are frightened in the presence of God.

If we have faith without works, we do not have saving faith. If we shared our faith with those we believe are lost, our churches would be overflowing. But we are not doing that. We say we believe, but we don't. We are not proving it by our lives. We are just giving lip-service to it. If we were asked if we believe in prayer, we would be insulted by the question. Of course we believe in prayer. But how much time do we spend in prayer? How important is that time when we shut the door, turn off the television, get away from the family and with our Bible to communicate with God?

We say we believe, but James says that if a man says he believes and his life doesn't prove it, he doesn't really believe. We rarely have a burden to see people saved. There is little urgency in our prayers. There is scarce necessity for our study time with God.

If I tell my wife I love her and never go home or provide her with any of the necessities, do you think she would believe me? I could keep telling her every day that I love her, but I must prove my love with my actions. We have created an entire culture of Christianity in America where we say we believe things that we are not practicing. If we believe in doing God's will, then let us do it. We do what we want to do. We are so frustrated because we are trying to please ourselves instead of God. We are trying to get what we want. We pay lip-service to Christianity and still expect blessings from it. We want to be blessed, but don't care anything about being a blessing.

THE CONDUCT

"Don't you remember that even our father Abraham was declared good because of what he *did,* when he was willing to obey God, even if it meant offering his son Isaac to die on the altar? You see, he was trusting God so much that he was willing to do whatever God told him to; his faith was made complete by what he did, by his actions, his good deeds. And so it happened just as the Scriptures say, that Abraham trusted God, and the Lord declared him good in God's sight, and he was even called 'the friend of God.' So you see, a man is saved by what he does as well as by what he believes. Rahab, the prostitute, is another example of this. She was saved because of what she did when she hid those messengers and sent them safely away by a different road. Just as the body is dead when there is no spirit in it, so faith is dead if it is not the kind that results in good deeds" (2:21-26).

James talks about Abraham's being justified by works by offering Isaac (Genesis 22). When he talks about Abraham's believing God and having it imputed to him for righteousness, he is referring to Genesis 15. Genesis 22 came forty years after Genesis 15. Forty years after he trusted God, after he declared his belief in God, after he was called a friend of God, he sacrificed his son and vindicated his faith. He proved that he meant it. If we read Genesis 22 carefully, we will discover that when God saw Abraham's obedience he said, "I will not require your son because now I know that you fear me, that you meant what you said back in Genesis 15."

Abraham said he believed God, then he proved it. God had promised to make a great nation out of Abraham through Isaac; yet God told him to kill Isaac. How much faith do you think it took for Abraham to sacrifice the promise God had given to him? It took so much faith that according to Hebrews 11, Abraham believed that if he killed Isaac, God would resurrect him.

We don't get a faith like that just by talking about it. Abraham had the kind of faith that said, "I believe God! I trust God with my life, my children, my future, my reputation." And God tested him. His obedience could cost him his reputation, his standing in the community. He would lose everything he had worked all of his life to maintain in the way of credibility, integrity, and character. But Abraham, trusting God with his character and his reputation, raised the knife to sacrifice his son. The Scripture says "he offered up . . ." (Hebrews 11:17, KJV), past tense. In his mind it was done. He said he believed God, and his life proved it. He risked everything in order to prove his faith.

So we see how by works a man is "justified." A faith that is only something we talk about doesn't vindicate anyone. Works reveal saving faith. A saving faith is a working faith. If we will read carefully the passages in the New Testament relative to predestination and foreordination, we will find that almost without exception they refer to how we are to live. We are ordained of God to live as a Christian ought to live.

James uses Rahab the harlot as another illustration of this principle. Here was a woman who was probably a prostitute in a pagan religion, a priestess or a prophetess in a pagan temple. Immorality was a part of the worship of their pagan gods. This woman, seeing the hand of God on the Israelites, went against the command of the leaders of her city and harbored the spies. She protected them and helped them to escape. She had faith and proved it. In the first chapter of Matthew, the lineage of Jesus, mentions a woman by the name of "Rachab" (KJV). Most scholars agree that it was Rahab, lifted from the doldrums of paganism to the lineage of the Messiah because she had a faith that linked her with God. And her life proved her faith.

James says, "Just as the body is dead when there is no spirit in it, so faith is dead if it is not the kind that results in good deeds" (2:26). I remember so vividly when they opened the casket and I saw my father's body. There was in my heart an overwhelming sense that it was not he. Something was missing. He wasn't there! A body without a spirit is useless. The body without the spirit is dead, barren, useless; so is faith without works. If a man says he has faith but there is no spirit in his faith, no life, no evidence, his faith is dead.

If we are saved, our lives will show it. If faith is only something we talk about, it is dead.

13

Our Great
Danger
James 3:1, 2

"DEAR BROTHERS, don't be too eager to tell others their faults, for we all make many mistakes; and when we teachers of religion, who should know better, do wrong, our punishment will be greater than it would be for others. If anyone can control his tongue, it proves that he has perfect control over himself in every other way" (James 3:1, 2).

This passage of Scripture deals primarily with what we say, how we speak. James begins by talking about teachers in the church. In the early church, the teacher was a very vital person. In Paul's epistles, we find that the teacher is placed in the same category as prophets, apostles, and pastors. They are all linked together as being very significant.

In the early church, the teacher was the one who taught the new converts. The teacher had the opportunity to pour his life into these new believers. The prophets and the apostles were basically itinerant; they moved from place to place. But the teacher was planted in the local congregation.

So it is to this group that James is talking here. He is pursuing another aspect of faith and works. Words are themselves works. We are able to see what a person believes by what he says. If we have received Christ into our hearts, it will affect how we speak. Jesus told the Phari-

sees, "You must give account on Judgment Day for every
idle word you speak. Your words now reflect your fate
then: either you will be justified by them or you will be
condemned" (Matthew 12:36, 37). Our words reveal our
true character.

We must guard and protect our words. Proverbs reminds us, "Whoso keepeth his mouth and his tongue
keepeth his soul from troubles" (21:23, KJV). In another
place, we read that death and life are in the power of the
tongue (Proverbs 18:21). Throughout the book of Proverbs
we are reminded that we are to guard and weigh very
carefully the words that we speak. That is good advice for
all of us, but especially for the teacher.

A DANGEROUS AMBITION

"Be not many masters [teachers]" (3:1, KJV). In other
words, everyone does not have the call of God to be a
teacher. Apparently, in the early church some sought the
honor and prestige given to the teacher, but did not want
to pay the price to be the kind of teacher that God can use.

The very sternest words Jesus ever spoke concerned
those who cherished the prestige of being teachers. Jesus
said concerning the scribes and Pharisees, "You would
think these Jewish leaders and these Pharisees were
Moses, the way they keep making up so many laws! And
of course you should obey their every whim! It may be all
right to do what they say, but above everything else, *don't
follow their example.* For they don't do what they tell you to
do. They load you with impossible demands that they
themselves don't even try to keep. Everything they do is
done for show. They act holy by wearing on their arms
little prayer boxes with Scripture verses inside, and by
lengthening the memorial fringes of their robes. And how

they love to sit at the head table at banquets, and in the reserved pews in the synagogue! How they enjoy the deference paid them on the street and to be called 'Rabbi' and 'Master' " (Matthew 23:2-7). They loved the prestige of being teachers, but didn't live what they taught.

James is not saying that no one should be a teacher, but that those whom God has called to teach need to realize that it is not a reward for their piety and holiness. It is a calling of God; and if a man is called, he needs to accept the tremendous responsibility that goes along with it.

A teacher will be judged by a more strict judgment than the person who listens (3:2). We who tell other people how to live are going to be held in very serious judgment by how *we* live. There are two great warnings here for a teacher. First, he needs to be sure he is teaching the truth. Second, he needs to be sure he practices what he teaches.

By virtue of the office, a teacher is always forming opinions and passing judgment. James is warning those who have deeper insight into the ways of God that they will be judged according to every insight they have. The more we learn things spiritually, the more we are held responsible. Every time we fail to practice a God-given insight, we will slide backwards spiritually. God holds us accountable for what we understand, for the enlightenment we have.

Many times we are concerned because we cannot understand something. But we will never understand some things until we start living up to the light we have, until we start practicing what we do understand. We try to understand the mysteries of life and death, tragedy and crisis, disappointment and heartache without even taking the first step in Christian obedience. No wonder we don't understand.

The difference between the person who experiences tragedy victoriously and the person who is plunged into deepest despair by the same tragedy is that one person is living up to the light and understanding he has, while the other is living in rebellion against what he knows. Those who are teachers have a greater responsibility and will receive a stricter judgment because of their greater enlightenment.

James is not talking about the eternal destiny of our souls. Jesus talks about the Christian not coming into condemnation (John 5:24). James does say that we will receive a stricter or greater condemnation, but if we look at the context we will see that he is not denying the certainty of our eternal destiny. We who believe in the security of the believer have been always accused of getting saved and then living as we want to. We do not believe that at all, and the Bible doesn't teach it. Once we have been saved, we have a responsibility to live out in our lives that which God has revealed to us.

What does this condemnation mean? It does not mean loss of salvation, but refers to the judgment-seat of Christ, a judgment of the Christian. Paul describes this judgment in 1 Corinthians 3:11-15. The basis of it all is Jesus Christ, the cornerstone, the foundation upon which we build. We shall appear before the judgment-seat of Christ so that our works may be judged, whether they be wood, hay, and stubble, or gold, silver, and precious stones. If they have been superfluous, they will be burned away because even the Christian is responsible for the way he lives. This judgment-seat is not to determine whether one goes to heaven or hell, but to determine the value and the nature of the life he has lived. The same concept is found in Romans, where we are told that every one of us must give an account of himself to God (Romans 14:10-12).

We shall receive a more stern judgment from God because he has enlightened us and told us how to live. Everything God impresses upon our hearts through his Word is to be put into practice in our lives.

A DELIBERATE ACCUSATION

" . . . for we all make many mistakes" (3:2). "Make many mistakes" speaks of carelessness. Most of our sins are not sins we plot; most of them are like going down steps. When we don't look, we stumble and fall. We commit them before we realize it. Our greatest rebellion against God is not a premeditated, deliberate affront to his Word, but careless treatment of what he has revealed to us.

We do that in many ways. The word "offend" (KJV) speaks in the Greek of repeated action. We continually stumble and slip up. If we err once a day, that amounts to almost 20,000 times in fifty years. But truthfully we sin more than once a day. In fact, we continually stumble.

We do this with our thoughts, with our actions, but most commonly with our tongue. The easiest sin to commit is a sin of the tongue, but it carries with it the harshest judgment. Three of the seven things that God hates (Proverbs 6:19) have to do with sins of the tongue.

A DISCIPLINED ACTION

"If anyone can control his tongue, it proves that he has perfect control over himself in every other way" (3:2). We can tell how strong and healthy spiritually we are by what we say. If we go to the doctor and tell him we don't feel well, the first thing he wants to look at is our tongue. If there is some problem, it may very well show by a coating on our tongue. And if he checks our temperature, he puts the thermometer under our tongue. Our tongue, physically, is a barometer of our health. The same thing is true spiritually. "Perfect" is a word which is used of a full-grown, mature person as opposed to a child or an infant. A mature person does not sin with his tongue. If we are able to bridle our tongue, it is evidence that we have our whole body under control.

Every teacher must guard his words. If we are not careful, we will give great pronouncements on social, economic, and religious subjects that we know nothing about. We think we know all the answers to all the political ills. The truth is that we have read three newspaper articles but don't really have an honest grasp of what is happening. We need to make sure that what we say is as true as it is possible for us to know from the Word of God. Our words must not be careless words.

The great themes that the teacher uses are subjects of immense value. We are dealing in eternity. We are talking about God, salvation, forgiveness of sins, the second coming, prophecy, the need of men to be saved, etc. We need to be careful that we choose, through God's leadership, the words that help us express these subjects accurately.

If we really know God, we want to teach the truth. Our danger as Christians is not deliberately teaching falsehood, but it is in being so negligent that we do not carefully and diligently seek out the truth before we say it. It is easy to be flippant. It is easy for us to pass over great truths as if they had no serious consideration at all.

The tongue is the hardest member of the body to control. We can control everything else more easily. We can control every aspect of our body if we can control our tongue.

Before James goes into a lesson on the tongue and its destructive nature and power, he stops at the very start to say that those of us who are faithful in the church and are given positions of responsibility are to take these responsibilities seriously. Great responsibility goes along with honor and esteem.

14

Mastering
the Tongue
James 3:3-12

"WE CAN MAKE a large horse turn around and go wherever we want by means of a small bit in his mouth. And a tiny rudder makes a huge ship turn wherever the pilot wants it to go, even though the winds are strong. So also the tongue is a small thing, but what enormous damage it can do. A great forest can be set on fire by one tiny spark. And the tongue is a flame of fire. It is full of wickedness, and poisons every part of the body. And the tongue is set on fire by hell itself, and can turn our whole lives into a blazing flame of destruction and disaster. Men have trained, or can train, every kind of animal or bird that lives and every kind of reptile and fish, but no human being can tame the tongue. It is always ready to pour out its deadly poison. Sometimes it praises our heavenly Father, and sometimes it breaks out into curses against men who are made like God. And so blessing and cursing come pouring out of the same mouth. Dear brothers, surely this is not right! Does a spring of water bubble out first with fresh water and then with bitter water? Can you pick olives from a fig tree, or figs from a grape vine? No, and you can't draw fresh water from a salty pool" (3:3-12).

This is an unbelievable passage of Scripture. James is not writing to infidels, but to practicing Christians. He is not writing to the agnostic, the man in the world who is blaspheming God; he is writing to the church. This is a staggering passage on the tremendous need to master the tongue, to subdue it, to have dominion over it, to conquer and control it.

James is not saying that silence is golden, that we should remain silent. He is saying that we need to speak, but with control over our speech. There are many folks who just abstain from a thing rather than having the discipline and the dedication to let God use it under control. James is not dealing with withholding speech, but controlling and mastering the speech that we use.

THE CONTROL

Verses 3 and 4 describe control. James has already said that if a man is able to bridle his tongue, he is able to control his whole body. He continues that thought by using the example of a horse. With all of the strength and power that resides within his body, a horse is controlled by the wise use of a small bit placed in his mouth. The original language indicates that not only is the bit in his mouth, but the reins that would implement the bit. If we do not control the tongue, the rest of our discipline is worthless. Just as we control the horse with the bit and bridle, the control of our tongue gives our body control.

It may well be that some of our problems with personal discipline could be traced back to the fact that we haven't controlled the tongue. It has become an instrument of unhappiness, bitterness, and rebellion against God. It may be that some of us who have had difficulty acquiring physical discipline should ask God to help us control our tongue, and thus give us mastery over the rest of our body.

In verse 3, James pictures a ship in a storm. It is hard enough to guide a boat in and out of the harbor, but here is a ship driven by fierce winds. Even in the midst of a storm, the ship is guided by a tiny rudder. How are we going to make it through the storms of life, with fierce winds seeking to destroy us? What will keep us safe in the storm? What we say in the midst of our problems determines whether we will have victory or not. If we doubt God and despair during our trials, they will destroy us. But if we use our tongues to claim God's provision and to claim his promises for our lives, we will have victory. It is easy to praise God when the sun is shining. But what about when the roof is leaking, when things have collapsed around us, when difficulties come?

Several times in the first chapters of the book of Job, even though he was encouraged to curse God and to react wrongly, we read that Job did not sin with bitter or complaining words (Job 1:22; 2:10). It was his steadfast refusal to accuse God and his steadfast determination to praise God in the midst of his problems that led him to a tremendous discovery of God. "I had heard about you before, but now I have seen you" (Job 42:5). In the midst of the storm, his tongue became an instrument of blessing and praise to God.

THE CHAOS

Beginning in verse 5, we see chaos. James speaks of fire that is uncontrolled and animals that are untamed. Several years ago I led one of my neighbors out of her burning home. In the midst of the confusion in trying to get out, she had run toward the fire. A fire throws everything into turmoil. James likens the tongue to a fire.

"So also the tongue is a small thing, but what enormous damage it can do. A forest can be set on fire by one tiny spark" (3:5). These people would have understood this analogy because the barren, arid land of the desert was covered with scrub trees and brush. If a fire started, it would sweep across a whole mountainside before it could be stopped. A spark is such a little thing, but it can start such great devastation. The tongue is like that.

Fire that is controlled is good. With controlled fire, we heat our houses, cook our meals, etc. There is a beauty and a warmth about a fire in its proper place. But a fire out of control is the worst imaginable thing. It destroys everything good and lovely in our lives. The tongue out of control does the same. The words that we speak have tremendous impact, so we must be careful how we use them.

"And the tongue is a flame of fire" (3:6). A forest fire sweeping across an arid desert land would burn everything in sight. So it is with our words. Our words have wide ranging effects. I can say a word in Euless, Texas, and affect a man in New York, San Francisco, or Miami for good or ill.

Think for a moment of the fire of a rumor. The headlines of the newspaper tell some great accusation against someone. The next day the back page has a retraction, but the damage cannot be undone. We are all guilty of drawing conclusions based upon poor information or basing a judgment on emotional issues with no basis in fact.

There is chaos from the wrong use of the tongue. James calls it "a world of iniquity" (KJV), but in the original language it is "*the* world of iniquity." There is in this world a spirit of rebellion against God. Whether we fail to say things we should or say things we should not have said, we give entrance into our bodies to a world of iniquity which "poisons every part of the body."

The hands, eyes, feet have some limitations, but not the tongue. We can violate every commandment of God with the tongue. With the tongue we can profane, blaspheme, and curse God. With the tongue we can steal, for we can take from our neighbor reputation or honor. With the tongue we can inflict great injury and suffering on those about us. With our tongue we can reveal infinite passion and lust. There is no sin that our tongue cannot commit.

"Men have trained, or can train, every kind of animal or bird that lives and every kind of reptile and fish" (3:7). This is not to say that every animal has been tamed, but every kind of animal has been subdued. In creation, God gave man dominion over all the created animal universe. Isn't it strange that man, who was given dominion over the universe, has lost dominion over his own body? He has lost control over himself and indeed all else.

"But no human being can tame the tongue. It is always ready to pour out its deadly poison" (3:8). No man can do it, but there is One who can. Our Lord Jesus can take a blasphemous tongue and turn it into a tongue of praise for God. Our Lord Jesus can take a gossipy, critical tongue and turn it into one of encouragement and blessing. Do not say, "It is just my nature; I cannot help it." No, but God can.

There is incredible potential in the tongue. With our tongues we can bless God and praise him. With our words we can express love and gratitude to God, we can encourage those who are discouraged, we can lift the spirits of those who are confused, we can bring comfort to those who are sorrowful, we can bring healing to those who are injured. The tongue can be a channel of blessing if we turn it over to Christ.

Christian faith and an uncontrolled tongue are incompatible. "Anyone who says he is a Christian but doesn't control his sharp tongue is just fooling himself, and his religion isn't worth much" (1:26).

"It is always ready to pour out its deadly poison" (3:8). With our tongue we can kill that which is right. We don't have to drink a lot of poison to die. Just a drop or two will kill. And we don't have to deliver a tirade against someone else; just a word here and a word there will do it. The tongue used in the wrong way will kill purity and faith in

God. It will kill trust in man, mutual affection among friends. It will destroy peace in a family and cut out the very life of the church if it is not controlled by the power of God.

THE CONTRADICTION

"Sometimes it praises our heavenly Father, and sometimes it breaks out into curses against men who are made like God. And so blessing and cursing come pouring out of the same mouth. Dear brothers, surely this is not right! Does a spring of water bubble out first with fresh water and then with bitter water? Can you pick olives from a fig tree, or figs from a grape vine? No, and you can't draw fresh water from a salty pool" (3:9-12). God despises inconsistency, and nowhere is our inconsistency more readily seen than in the use of our tongues. Some of the most graciously uttered prayers, some of the most skillfully delivered sermons have been spoken by people who later used their words to destroy someone they didn't like. Here is a contradiction; the tongue that ought to be praising God is also cursing men. "Praise" means to express love and gratitude. We bless God and then curse men made after the image of God. Actually if we condemn them or invoke evil upon men, we are ultimately cursing God.

"Dear brothers, surely this is not right!" (3:10). It is abnormal to bless God and curse man. It is contrary both to grace and to nature. It cannot be.

The tongue is our greatest opportunity for good and the greatest threat for evil in our lives. "No man can tame the tongue"; we can never take it off the leash. Our tongues must always be in check. Unless it is under God's control, it will strike out. The mastery of our tongues is only possible through our Lord Jesus Christ.

15 Wisdom from Above
James 3:13-18

"If you are wise, live a life of steady goodness, so that only good deeds will pour forth. And if you don't brag about them, then you will be truly wise! And by all means don't brag about being wise and good if you are bitter and jealous and selfish; that is the worst sort of lie. For jealousy and selfishness are not God's kind of wisdom. Such things are earthly, unspiritual, inspired by the devil. For wherever there is jealousy or selfish ambition, there will be disorder and every other kind of evil. But the wisdom that comes from heaven is first of all pure and full of quiet gentleness. Then it is peace-loving and courteous. It allows discussion and is willing to yield to others; it is full of mercy and good deeds. It is wholehearted and straightforward and sincere. And those who are peacemakers will plant seeds of peace and reap a harvest of goodness" (3:13-18).

True wisdom is the ability to live a beautiful life, to put into practice what we say we believe and teach. "Let him shew out of a good conversation his works with meekness of wisdom" (3:13, KJV). The word "conversation" years ago referred not to our words, but to the way we lived, and this is the way it is used here. A man who is truly wise will show by his conduct that what he says is true. "Good" means "splendid" or "noble." To James, religion was more than just beautiful words.

"Meekness" does not mean weakness. Indeed, no man can truly be meek unless he really knows his strength. Meekness is controlled power, energy harnessed for the glory of God. James reminds us that there is no real wisdom without meekness.

FALSE WISDOM

Beginning in verse 14, James deals with false wisdom. Its first characteristic is "bitter envying" (KJV). This is an interesting combination of words. "Envy" is the Greek word *zelos* from which we get our word "zeal." Zeal is a good thing if it is channelled in the right direction and put to the right purpose. But here we see "bitter zeal." This pictures a spirit of harsh resentment, someone who cannot bear to see someone else succeed. Some will do anything they can to hurt or humiliate someone else who receives a degree of success. Their hearts are filled with jealousy and anger.

James ties "bitter envyings" to "strife in your hearts." This describes one who selfishly divides a group into factions deliberately trying to create divisions.

Notice that James begins by talking about what is in our hearts, and not our outward works. What we do comes from what we are in our hearts. When we are wrong in our hearts, we will be wrong in our lives and wrong with our words. This deals with motives.

"That is the worst sort of lie" (3:14). When we have the kind of spirit described above and we preach the truth, our lives are denying the very truth that we are proclaiming. We are living a lie. False wisdom leads one to say, "Do as I say, not as I do." Whenever the church can confront this world with people whose lives are consistent with what they say, revival will be on its way.

"For jealousy and selfishness are not God's kind of

wisdom. Such things are earthly, unspiritual, inspired by the devil" (3:15). "Earthly" simply means that false wisdom is based upon earthly standards, earthly sources, earthly aims—and measures itself by earthly success. "Unspiritual" means opposed to God, anything that is normal to us but not normal to God. It is the natural man as opposed to the supernatural God. False wisdom is the outgrowth of man's energies and man's imagination. It is "inspired by the devil." That ought to frighten us. Whenever we are guilty of having the spirit described in these verses, we are being influenced by demonic forces. So, a bad attitude is not just a shame; it is something Satan is fostering in our lives.

"For wherever there is jealousy or selfish ambition, there will be disorder and every other kind of evil" (3:16). Wherever the wisdom of the world is demonstrated, there is confusion and disorder. "God is not the one who likes things to be disorderly and upset" (1 Corinthians 14:13). Wherever there is confusion, Satan is at the source of it, not God. Such an attitude as James has described leads to every conceivable kind of evil: immorality, dishonesty, discord. Nothing good can grow in such an atmosphere as that.

TRUE WISDOM

Then, in contrast to the false wisdom, James lists the characteristics of true wisdom. "But the wisdom that comes from heaven is first of all pure . . ." (3:17). "Pure" means without alloy, with no disposition toward evil, free from taint.

" . . . and full of quiet gentleness." We cannot translate "gentleness" adequately, but it means "reasonable" or "considerate." It forgives even when the letter of the law says to condemn. Can you imagine what the fellowship of the church would be like if that were the spirit in which we related to each other?

Then it is "peace-loving." Real wisdom produces right relationships, with man and with God. True wisdom would lead us to build a peaceable spirit which is not contentious, but is a spirit of peace and love with each other and with God.

"It allows discussion and is willing to yield to others" ("easy to be entreated," KJV). That last phrase is one word in the Greek language and depicts one who readily and happily submits to discipline, particularly military discipline. It describes a soldier who is happy to obey orders. Real wisdom will lead us to be joyfully disciplined by the Spirit of God.

This wisdom is also "full of mercy and good deeds." Real wisdom is a compassionate wisdom; it produces kind acts toward others.

Real wisdom is "wholehearted." That means that it is unwavering, uncompromising. It speaks of one who knows the truth and stands upon it in a "straightforward and sincere" ("without hypocrisy," KJV) manner.

We can study for hours the meaning of this wisdom from heaven. In light of what is described here, each of us ought to go to our knees to ask God, through his Spirit, to produce this wisdom in us.

"And the fruit of righteousness is sown in peace of them that make peace" (3:18, KJV). Notice that James did not say that the *seed* of righteousness is sown, but rather the "fruit" of righteousness. There is no question in his mind that there is going to be a crop, that what they sow they will harvest. "The fruit of righteousness is sown in peace." Those who seek righteousness seek peace peaceably. Those who are peaceable in their hearts sow the fruit of righteousness and thus make peace.

Peace is not natural in this world. It is not a natural consequence in a world of sin and evil. Jesus Christ came to make peace. By his death on the cross and by his resurrection, he tore down the wall and made peace. Do we find in ourselves bitter envyings and strife? Do we find in ourselves confusion and evil works? Of course we do! That is when we need to yield it all to God, confess it to him, and ask for that wisdom that is from above.

We don't have to ask for worldly wisdom. We don't have to teach our children to rebel. We never have to teach a child to say "no," or to cry and want his way. It is natural. But if we are to have true wisdom, we must ask for it. We will have to seek that wisdom that is from above. When that becomes the passion of our lives, the fruit of righteousness will be sown in us and through us to those around us.

The Source
of Conflicts
James 4:1-3

16

"WHAT IS CAUSING the quarrels and fights among you?
Isn't it because there is a whole army of evil desires within
you? You want what you don't have, so you kill to get it.
You long for what others have, and can't afford it, so you
start a fight to take it away from them. And yet the reason
you don't have what you want is that you don't ask God
for it. And even when you do ask you don't get it because
your whole aim is wrong—you want only what will give
you pleasure" (4:1-3).

When we come to James 4, it seems as if we run right
into a brick wall. We close the third chapter talking
about the fruit of righteousness sown in peace. Then
immediately we come to a picture of war, confusion, and
distress. Bear in mind that this book is addressed to
Christians.

"What is causing the quarrels and fights among you?"
James is not talking about strife between nations, or about
natural enmity between God's people and the pagan
world. He is not talking about the frustration, strife, con-
tention, and war that exists outside the Christian community. He is speaking about those who claim to know
Jesus Christ. God's people were never designed or created to live like that.

"Quarrels" speaks of feuds and continuous conflict.

In addition, James refers to long drawn-out resentment, and a spirit of bitterness and anger toward others, God, or life in general. This is a spirit of conflict within the heart. "Fights" does not refer to continuous warfare or a general conflict, but of individual conflicts. It speaks of a sudden explosion rather than a long period of resentment.

Where does all this come from? It is important for us to discover the answer to this because across America today there is as much conflict within the church as there is outside it. That is why Christianity limps along and why there are such sad caricatures of Christians. A godless world looks in and sees nothing different than what they see outside. Why is there such continuous warfare within the church? God did not intend for it to be that way. God is not the author of such a spirit. If we can discover the source of these conflicts and the things that tear us apart, maybe we can deal with them.

PLEASURE
In verse 1, James reveals that the first source is a natural craving for pleasure. "Isn't it because there is a whole army of evil desires within you?" The Greek word translated "evil desires" is the word from which we get "hedonism," which means an unbridled search for pleasure. This philosophy is based on what pleases me. That drive for pleasure is constantly carrying on a war in our members.

He is *not* saying that this drive for pleasure is causing conflict between two individuals in the church. It is "within you." Every conflict we have begins within us: in our bodies, in our minds, in our emotions. There is a continuous state of war within us. The Apostle Paul described this in detail in Romans 7. We who belong to Jesus Christ must be obedient to God or our physical being, our emotions, and all that we are will lose a spiritual battle. Such a spirit of war and fighting comes to us because we seek to please ourselves.

Why does such a spirit create dissension? Because we can please ourselves only at another's expense.

Every part of life is a battleground. There is a war taking place for our minds right now. There is a battle raging for our emotions every day. There is a battle raging for our strengths and our energies, for our dreams and our visions. Our bodies are battlefields.

Pleasure-seeking destroys our love for spiritual things. We may still keep on doing them, but we do them out of duty and not love. Jesus said, "Wear my yoke—for it fits perfectly—and let me teach you; for I am gentle and humble, and you shall find rest for your souls; for I give you only light burdens" (Matthew 11:29, 30). When we love Jesus, the easiest and most joyful thing in the world is to serve him and obey him. But when the goal of our lives is obtaining selfish pleasures, our obedience becomes simply a disagreeable duty.

Some of us go to church out of a sense of obligation. We have become so preoccupied with becoming "spiritual" that we have forgotten that the real mark of spirituality is to love Jesus. If we love Jesus with all of our being, we will be spiritual Christians. Religious ritual, Christian service out of duty and not out of love, destroys our relationship with the Lord.

So the conflicts in our lives come because of a passion for pleasure. If we have conflicts and problems, we have no one else to blame but ourselves. If our homes are not running smoothly, it is easier for the husband to blame the wife or the wife to blame the husband, but the source of conflict is within *us*. It is *our* spirit, *our* attitude. It is innate selfishness within us that wants to be pleased and pampered. We must face the truth.

PASSION

"Want" (4:2) is the word *epithumea,* which means "longing to possess." It speaks of envy, a longing to possess certain things (generally material things or physical things that we can touch or feel). We desire to have what we cannot obtain. What a graphic picture of frustration! God is telling us that the wrong desire in our heart will not be fulfilled.

"You kill to get it . . . you start a fight to take it. . . ." Some say that James did not mean that we actually commit murder. However, the original language clearly says "kill" or "murder." There is a deep passion in our lives that will find expression in some way, either for God or for the pleasure of the world. In our frustration we strike out in wars and fightings and we will even kill to get what we want. Yet when we have done it all, we still won't have what we want.

There has never been one time when Satan has ever delivered what he promised. There has never been one time when a man received satisfaction and happiness from living in rebellion against God. Not once! But we don't believe it. Somehow we think we are the exception. We are dishonest in our businesses or in our homes. We divorce and remarry. And we pay the price.

We don't have satisfaction because we are looking in the wrong place. There are many who think God is the super killjoy, the original wet blanket. They think he doesn't want anybody to have fun or to be happy. How wrong they are. God wants us to be happy. God has a great sense of humor. God wants us to be happy and smile. He wants us to come alive. He sent Jesus Christ to suffer hell for us so we wouldn't have to suffer it. It is not wrong to want to be pleased and satisfied, but it is wrong to seek it in the wrong ways. We must let God place in our lives the ingredients of happiness.

Suppose I invited you to my house for dessert. Then I told you that we were going to have angel food cake and I was going to make it, and I told you I would use a little pancake mix, some baking soda, a couple of brownie mixes, some water, milk, and vinegar. You would think I was crazy. Those ingredients would never make an angel food cake. Why can't I make it the way I want to? I can't make angel food cake with just any ingredients.

God says, "Love me and obey me, and I will give you such happiness that you can hardly bear it." But we say to God, "I want to do it my way. I will mix in a little anger and hostility, a little sex and some narcotics, plus a little pride and arrogance. Then I will be happy." No, that will create hell on earth.

We don't get happy because we try to be happy. We are happy when we ask God for happiness. In relationship with God, in obedience to him, in walking with him, we find happiness. If we do not bring our desire for satisfaction to God, then we will bring it to Satan and he will pervert it and destroy us. When the passion of our lives becomes pleasure at any cost, satisfaction upon demand, "I'll do it my way," God says, "You don't have what you want because you haven't come to me."

Some of us say, "Now wait a minute. I asked God for something and didn't get it. I did everything he told me to and I didn't feel anything. It didn't work." James answers that by saying, "And even when you do ask you don't get it because your whole aim is wrong—you want only what will give *you* pleasure" (4:3). Sometimes we ask for the wrong reasons, out of a selfish desire to satisfy our own pleasure. We may ask for something that is good, but if we don't ask for the right reasons, we will not receive it. I have known of Christian athletes who have prayed that they could win, so God could get the glory. That is possible, but there is a very fine line between wanting God to get the glory for a victory and just wanting the victory. We must be careful that we are not praying selfishly.

PATTERN

This passage also shows us a pattern of evil conduct. We can avoid many of the sins that are in our lives if we watch the danger signs. We lust and have not. We desire to have and cannot obtain. So we kill and fight and war. Here is how sin begins in our lives: with a desire. It could be a desire for money, sex, achievement, etc. It may be a desire for something that belongs to someone else.

Then we begin to think about it and before we know it, it consumes our thoughts. It crowds and occupies our minds. We dream about it at night, we wake up thinking about it in the morning, until finally that desire becomes a controlling passion in our lives. Whenever our desires for pleasure and satisfaction begin to control our lives, war and fighting will result. If we think about immorality enough, we can be sure we will commit it. That is why we are to flee youthful lusts and every appearance of evil. Once Satan has planted a desire in our hearts, if we do not yield it up to the Father, it will become a driving passion that will ultimately end in disaster.

Our conflicts within, our conflicts with each other, and our lack of satisfaction go back to one thing: we will either please ourselves or we will please God. We have one ultimate choice: are we going to live for ourselves, trying to satisfy every desire, greed and passion in our lives, or will we live for God?

Jesus said, "For anyone who keeps his life for himself shall lose it; and anyone who loses his life for me shall find it again" (Matthew 16:25). We can only keep what we give to God. Everything we try to keep we will lose. If we give our possessions to God, he will transfer them into eternal securities. If we give our children to God, he will give them back to us. Whatever we give to him, we will receive back from him many times over.

Friendship
with the
World
James 4:4, 5

"YOU ARE LIKE an unfaithful wife who loves her husband's enemies. Don't you realize that making friends with God's enemies—the evil pleasures of this world—makes you an enemy of God? I say it again, that if your aim is to enjoy the evil pleasure of the unsaved world, you cannot also be a friend of God. Or what do you think the Scripture means when it says that the Holy Spirit, whom God has placed within us, watches over us with tender jealousy?" (4:4, 5).

INFIDELITY

James begins with the accusation, "You are like an unfaithful wife." Our first reaction might be that this passage does not apply to us because we are not adulterous. But James is talking about spiritual adultery, spiritual infidelity. He is speaking about a Christian who betrays his faith, who denies his Lord.

This goes back to the Old Testament picture of God as the husband of Israel. ". . . for your Creator will be your 'husband.' The Lord of Hosts is his name; he is your Redeemer, the Holy One of Israel, the God of all the earth" (Isaiah 54:5). Whenever God's people went into idolatry, they were being unfaithful to God. Thus, idolatry was adultery.

In this passage, James is giving us Christian interpretation of Old Testament truth. When we become friends with the world, we are committing spiritual adultery. If we claim to know God, but deny the faith by refusing to do what God has called us to do, we are unfaithful.

God has entered into a relationship with us (see verse 5). When we sin, we violate that relationship. Our response to God is a response of love, not law. Our relationship to God is not just one of a king to a servant, but of a husband to a wife—a relationship of intimacy, friendship, and love.

Therefore, when we violate our vows to God, we are not just sinning against law, but against love. It is one thing to break the law and another thing to break the heart of someone who loves you. God has loved us intensely and has given to us his son, Jesus Christ. When we resist him, we are rebelling against his love.

If a son walked up to his father and hit him and cursed him, we would consider him a terrible person. How do you suppose God feels when we, who have been redeemed by his love, treat him with rebellion and ingratitude? This is spiritual adultery.

"Don't you realize that making friends with God's enemies—the evil pleasures of this world—makes you an enemy of God?" (3:4). Friendship with the world is enmity with God. We need to understand that James is not just talking about adopting a lifestyle of evil. We think that if we are in league with the world, we would live like the world. We would commit dishonesty, immorality, murder. But that is not necessarily involved in friendship with the world. There sometimes comes a time in our spiritual lives when we feel comfortable with people who don't love God, with forces that are ungodly. They may not be hostile to God; they may simply be indifferent to him. James declares that if we hold friendship with that kind of people, we are enemies of God.

One of the great tragedies today is that the church feels

so much at home in the world. It doesn't bother us when we see dishonesty and vulgarity. We hear others taking God's name in vain and are not offended. We may not necessarily *do* the things of the world, but we accept what they do and have become comfortable with it.

We sometimes think that as long as we don't openly rebel against God, we are all right. But God says, "If you are comfortable and settled into a relationship with the world, you are hostile toward me." At any point where we have a friendship with the world, where we have a partnership with those who disregard God, we are hostile toward God.

It is important to note that our enmity toward God does not make God stop loving us. He still cares about us. Nowhere is the love of God seen more clearly or more forcefully than when his people reject him and establish infidelity as a practice of life. The hostility is always one way. God is never hostile toward us. He judges our sin, but he loves us.

Think of how many times we failed to do something we knew God wanted us to do because there was something we considered more important. It may not have been something that was necessarily anti-God. It might have been a football game that meant more to us than our fellowship with God's people or our worship. That is certainly not wrong in itself. But when it crowds out God, we are being hostile toward him.

One of the things that has happened in our time is that we no longer draw the line. We have so much world in the church and so much church in the world that we have a hard time telling the two apart. We have tried to have the best of both worlds.

"I say it again, that if your aim is to enjoy the evil pleasure of the unsaved world, you cannot also be a friend of God" (4:4). We can see from the original Greek construction that James is talking about a deliberate choice. A

Christian may find himself in hostile surroundings, in the middle of people who do not love God. That is one thing. But to *choose* to be a friend of the world is to become an enemy of God.

It is even more tragic when we are God's enemies and do not even care. Some of us act nice on Sunday, but live like the world through the week. No one in the world knows we have given our lives to Christ. We carry on business during the week with no evidence of belonging to God. But we are either for him or against him. We are either God's friends or friends with the world. God continually calls us to be separate, to live lives of godliness, and to identify with Christ. Many of us know what Simon Peter went through when he cursed and said, "I don't know Christ." Too few of us know what he went through when he went out and wept bitterly and repented.

What does it mean to be a friend of the world? James has already mentioned four things. He has talked about a spirit of discord within the fellowship of God's people. Wherever one creates discord in the fellowship of the church, that person is an enemy of God. He has talked about the empty life, the life of frustration. He has spoken about an untamed tongue. That is ungodliness and friendship with the world. He has talked about a jealous heart and an envious spirit.

INDWELLING

"Or what do you think the Scripture means when it says that the Holy Spirit, whom God has placed within us, watches over us with tender jealousy?" (4:5).

God's Spirit dwells inside us. If we could just discover the excitement and the reality of the truth of that great truth! The Christian's body houses the Holy Spirit. The

Holy Spirit longs to love through us and to live through us.

Next James tells us that the Holy Spirit is jealous. The Holy Spirit of God does not want us to give one ounce of our energy, one moment of our time, one square inch of our hearts to ungodly things. God's Spirit is jealous of every moment that is stolen from him. Every affection that is given to the world grieves him. He struggles for it and fights for it.

How much the Spirit of God works in us when we have done wrong! It is the Spirit of God who jealously guards us, bringing conviction so that we will not waste our lives. The Spirit of God does not want to give us up to the world and does not want to give us up to Satan. He jealously guards us.

It is a great encouragement to know that God is interested in everything we think, everything we do, everything that captures our imaginations, every word that we speak, every thought that comes into our minds. The Holy Spirit jealously guards what is his. "Know ye not that your body is the temple of the Holy Ghost . . . therefore glorify God in your body, and in your spirit, which are God's" (1 Corinthians 6:19, 20, KJV).

We have a choice. We can continue in a path of resistance to the purposes and will of God, be a friend of the world, and have a spirit within us of turmoil all the time. But no tranquilizer can soothe the conviction of the Holy Spirit; nothing can calm the heart that is in rebellion to God. Or we can choose to be God's friends and live in harmony with him.

We must realize that Christianity is a life. It is not just up for church and then doing as we please. It is a way of living, acting, dressing, walking, talking, and relating to other people. We must choose whether we will be friends of the world or friends with God.

Grace to the Humble
James 4:6-10

18

"BUT HE GIVES US more and more strength to stand against all such evil longings. As the Scripture says, God gives strength to the humble, but sets himself against the proud and haughty. So give yourselves humbly to God. Resist the devil and he will flee from you. And when you draw close to God, God will draw close to you. Wash your hands, you sinners, and let your hearts be filled with God alone to make them pure and true to him. Let there be tears for the wrong things you have done. Let there be sorrow and sincere grief. Let there be sadness instead of laughter, and gloom instead of joy. Then when you realize your worthlessness before the Lord, he will lift you up, encourage and help you" (4:6-10).

THE RESOURCES

"But he gives us more and more strength to stand against all such evil longings" (4:6). Whatever God demands of us, he provides the means by which we can produce it. Whatever demands of purity and holiness and whatever pressures the world may place upon us, James declares that God will give us enough grace for each moment. He

122

will not demand something of us that his grace cannot provide.

Even as Christians, it is impossible for us to conform to the standards of God, but God gives us what we need. Do we face the sadness and pressure of grief and sorrow? God's grace will give us enough strength, comfort, and fellowship to handle it. Do we face a tragedy that threatens to change the course of our lives? God will point us in the right direction. Is sin leaping up before us, seeking to force compromise on us? God will give us his grace.

We don't live by *our* resources; we live by his. Too often we try to do the best we can; we give God the best we have. We walk in our own strength. The key to victory in the Christian life is not living on our resources, but on his. He gives all that we need.

God "sets himself against the proud and haughty." "Proud" means "to show yourself above other people" or "to lift yourself up against others and against God." It speaks of an arrogant spirit that shakes its fist in the face of God and refuses to admit it needs him. This is an inward thing. It is possible for someone to look very sad, very meek, very humble on the outside but inwardly be arrogant.

The spirit of pride and arrogance attacks God, lifts itself up against him. God resists a person with that kind of spirit. Sadly, this kind of person does not recognize his own need. He is arrogant in his defense of himself in his opposition to God. God can do nothing with the person who will not allow him to do it.

God resists the proud, the one who arrogantly turns against him, but gives grace unto the humble. "Humble" is the opposite of "proud." It speaks of a person who recognizes his absolute dependence upon God, his need for the touch of God upon his life. That kind of person is one who will receive God's grace.

THE RESPONSE

"Give yourselves humbly to God. Resist the devil and he will flee from you. And when you draw close to God, God will draw close to you" (4:7, 8a). Our response to a God who loves us ought to be to surrender our lives to him, to place ourselves under his control. Most people's problems exist because they refuse to submit to the Lordship of Christ in their lives. The will of God is not like an Easter egg that is hidden so that we can't find it. Most of us know what we ought to do and how we ought to live, but we are not willing to do it. We are not willing to submit to the authority of God.

Secondly, we are to "resist" the devil. "Resist" is a defensive word. If someone is attacking us, we resist him. When we become saved, we not only receive a new Savior, but a new enemy. Whether we know it or not, Satan begins to bombard us with temptations and testings. We are now his enemy, we cannot be neutral. We cannot ride the fence. God says, "If you are going to respond to me, you must resist him." This requires diligent effort, sturdiness of character, a deep commitment to God that says, "I will stand for God."

Some think that Christian submission is a weak kind of thing that allows people to run rampant over it. They take the principles "turn the other cheek" and "go the extra mile" completely out of context and think that we become doormats for anyone that wants to steamroll over us. God says, "Resist the enemy. Stand up to him." "Resist" literally means "to stand up against." If we who are God's people would stand firm and resist Satan, we could change the course of our society.

The problems in America today, the corruption of our morality and our spiritual lives, the collapse of our homes and our economic system is to a great degree the fault of God's people. Don't blame the atheists and those who

JAMES
4:6-10

mock God. Anytime a group of God's people get serious about changing their society, God can use them to do just that. Our response to God is all-important. You see, Satan is a coward. He is vulnerable. When we stand on the Word of God and make it the pattern of our lives, Satan will flee from us.

Satan is not our problem. We are our problem. The closer we get to God, the more Satan tries to attack us; but the more we stand in the power of God, the more he flees from us in defeat. Most of us flirt with temptation and court evil, then wonder why we have problems. We are to stand in submission to God and in resistance to the devil and his forces. Then Satan will flee from us.

Please do not understand that to say that the closer we get to God, the less problem we will have with Satan. We will have many problems with him. The closer we get to God, the more Satan will attack us. But he can be resisted and he will flee. We do not have to submit to Satan. There is victory for us. Satan is a defeated foe. If we stand in the power of Christ, submitting ourselves to God, we will have victory over him.

Notice James says that "when you draw close to God, God will draw close to you." We couldn't possibly want to be close to God as much as he wants to be close to us. We couldn't possibly want to love God as much as he loves us. So when we don't feel as close to God as we once did, the problem does not lie with God. We have allowed compromise and evil to come into our lives. Isaiah said, "Listen now! The Lord isn't too weak to save you. And he isn't getting deaf! He can hear you when you call! But the trouble is that your sins have cut you off from God. Because of sin he has turned his face away from you and will not listen anymore" (Isaiah 59:1, 2). When we are drawn away from God, it is by our own choosing.

When we feel the presence of God and the drawing of

God in our lives, we need to act upon it. When we know that God is calling us to make a decision, we must do it. It is in his nearness that we find our greatest opportunity of blessing.

THE REPENTANCE

James gives us a five-fold description of repentance: "Wash your hands, you sinners, and let your hearts be filled with God alone to make them pure and true to him. Let there be tears for the wrong things you have done. Let there be sorrow and sincere grief. Let there be sadness instead of laughter, and gloom instead of joy" (4:8-10). Here, again, is a reminder to us of the high ethical standard that God sets for his children. "Wash" is a word that originally meant ceremonial cleansing, the washing of hands to prepare for the sacrifice. It referred to outward cleansing. Our bodies and our lives ought to be outwardly pure, outwardly holy. Our lives should not be involved in those things that bring discredit to the name of Christ. Wash the outside; cleanse what is seen.

But Christianity is not just a way of putting on an act or a front; it is a matter of the heart. "Purify your hearts ye double-minded" (4:8, KJV). "Double-minded" means "someone who cannot make up his mind." It pictures someone wavering between two opinions. A man who cleanses the outside and leaves the inside impure is a double-minded man. We are to cleanse our hands and purify our hearts. In our hearts we are to confess our sin and embrace the holiness and righteousness of God, allowing the presence of the Lord Jesus to fill our lives and control our heart.

"Let there be tears for the wrong things you have done. Let there be sorrow and sincere grief. Let there be sadness instead of laughter, and gloom instead of joy" (3:9). Bear in mind that James is talking about people who love the world, who are friends with the world, who have given deference to the rich, who have offended and oppressed the poor, who have given themselves to luxury and have lived in utter selfishness.

"Sorrow" ("afflicted," KJV) is a word used to describe an army that has run out of food, that has no place for shelter. James is saying, "You have made the luxury and comfort of this world the standard by which you judge your life. Don't do that! Be afflicted!" Christians cannot set their sights by the standards of the world. We are not to build our lives upon luxury, comfort, and ease. These things have come in abundance to us in America, and maybe that is why it is so difficult for us to be truly Christian in America. "Be afflicted" has the same root as the word the Apostle Paul uses when he says, "O *wretched* man that I am, who shall deliver me from the body of this death?" (Romans 7:24, KJV).

James tells us to have "sincere grief" ("mourn," KJV). We are to see ourselves as sinners. Knowing what sin does to a holy God should bring grief to our souls. We should weep because of the sin in our lives.

We should also mourn because there are people in the world who are grieving and sad. We need to be acquainted with their grief. We need to feel their sorrow and their sadness. This is a challenge to get outside ourselves and be a part of what God wants to do in the lives of others.

"Let there be sadness instead of laughter, and gloom instead of joy." Here James rebukes the flippant attitude with which some people approach spiritual things and the needs of those around them. He is talking about a shallow, hypocritical, self-righteous laughter. Life is serious. Though there is a deep-seated peace and joy that comes to us as God's children, we are not to take the needs of the world lightly.

THE REWARD

"Then when you realize your worthlessness before the Lord, he will lift you up, encourage and help you" (4:10). The person humbles himself when he is aware of the greatness of God and of his own insignificance and inadequacy. Recognizing his need and his insufficiency, he turns to a mighty God. "Before the Lord" ("in the sight of the Lord," KJV) means to see ourselves as God sees us. We must let God reveal to us what we are really like.

Some years ago, in one of the more crushing experiences of my life, I came to understand what it meant for Jesus to be Lord in my life. God cracked the door of my heart and let me look in and see what he had been looking at all along. I had always thought that I was purer than I was, that there were sins that I wouldn't commit. I thought there were things that would never come into my life. But that morning God let me look in, and I saw in my own heart the blackness of a thousand midnights and the seed of every sin known to man. God told me there was no sin that I would not commit. He let me see myself as he saw me. Out of the brokenness of my heart then emerged a wholeness that has brought immeasurable blessing to my life. Recognize the magnificence of God and let him show you yourself as he sees you.

When we do that, notice what happens: "He will lift you up, encourage and help you." Does that mean he will make all the poor rich, all the feeble strong, or all the ignorant wise? No, it means he will lift us up eternally. When a man gets elected to a political office, a few years pass, later he is defeated. He is elevated, then cast down. A man is a hero and then he is forgotten. But God elevates to eternal rewards.

He elevates us now in spirit, giving us peace in the midst of the turmoil of this life. He gives us forgiveness in the midst of terrible, unbearable guilt that most people carry. He gives us comfort in the midst of sorrow. He gives us wisdom in the midst of confusion. He gives us a purpose for living. He gives us contentment and peace in our hearts. That is what he does right now. But this will keep on until someday we will be with him and sit in heavenly places, ruling with him (Revelation 1:6). We will be elevated in his presence and kingdom. It all starts when we recognize his greatness and our need. Everything that Jesus Christ is, he will be in us if we turn to him in repentance and faith.

Watch Your
Language
James 4:11, 12

"DON'T CRITICIZE and speak evil about each other, dear brothers. If you do, you will be fighting against God's law of loving one another, declaring it is wrong. But your job is not to decide whether this law is right or wrong, but to obey it. Only he who made the law can rightly judge among us. He alone decides to save us or destroy. So what right do you have to judge or criticize others?" (4:11, 12).

James now proceeds to talk about the presumptuous pride that would cause someone to ridicule the law of God and set himself up as a judge.

THE PROHIBITION

Verse 11 commands us to refrain from speaking evil of each other. We are not to engage in slanderous talk against each other. It is not wrong for us to form opinions about people, but it is wrong for us to do it in an unkind or unjust way. The thing that is here condemned is not forming an opinion that says someone is wrong, but the love of fault finding.

We delight in finding something bad about someone else, particularly if we do not like them. But God, when he views our sins, views us with a broken heart. God has a heart of love.

Whether or not something is true is not a sufficient criterion to use in deciding whether or not to say it. Even if it is true, that does not give us the right to say it. If we say anything that would hurt someone else unnecessarily, then we are wrong in saying it.

We often think that such talk is a small thing. If we were classifying sins, it would be at the bottom of the list. But there are few sins that the Bible more uniformly condemns than this one. For example, look at Ephesians 4:31 and 1 Peter 2:1. The Psalmist has a great deal to say about this matter also. "I will not tolerate anyone who secretly slanders his neighbors; I will not permit conceit and pride" (Psalm 101:5). "Do you want a long, good life? Then watch your tongue! Keep your lips from lying" (Psalm 34:12, 13). And when the writer of Proverbs lists the seven things that God hates, at least two of them pertain to how we speak of each other (Proverbs 6:16-19).

I love the references throughout the New Testament to the "family of God." You have heard the expression, "Blood is thicker than water." We have been saved by the blood of Jesus Christ; it is his blood that brings forgiveness of sin. There ought to be in the fellowship of the Christian church a tie that is far stronger than any other could possibly be. It is the tie of the faith within the family of God. We belong to each other, and we ought to be sensitive to each other. We ought to care about each other. Hurtful speech within the fellowship of the faith is prohibited. "Don't criticize and speak evil about each other."

THE PRESUMPTION
"If you do, you will be fighting against God's law of loving one another, declaring it is wrong. But your job is not to decide whether this law is right or wrong, but to obey it. Only he who made the law can rightly judge among us. He alone decides to save us or destroy. So what right do

you have to judge or criticize others?" (4:11, 12) James speaks of a presumptuous person who would say he knows as much as God or is as important as God, evidenced by his judging other people. It is presumptuous for us to play God, but that is exactly what happens when a person brings evil accusations against another. "He that speaketh evil of his brother, and judgeth his brother, speaketh evil of the law, and judgeth the law" (KJV). In other words, he judges which part of the law applies to him.

Matthew 7:1-5 talks about how inexcusable it is for us to judge one another. It points out how ridiculous it is for a person with a beam in his eye to notice a speck of dust in another's eye. In Galatians 6:1-10, Paul talks about doing good and speaking well of all men, "especially those of the household of faith." Again, we are back to the family concept. If ever we ought to be kind to anyone, it ought to be to fellow-Christians.

Sometimes it seems that the Christian army is the only army in the world that buries its wounded. If someone is hurt, rather than being redemptive and restoring, we want to condemn them and beat them. We look for reasons to be unkind and critical. That is strictly forbidden. We are not only putting down others, but the law of God.

What law is James talking about? In particular, he is talking about the law God gave, the great law of Israel: "Love the Lord your God with all of your heart, soul, and mind. . . . Love your neighbor as much as you love yourself" (Matthew 22:35-38).

When we speak evilly of another, we violate God's law; we laugh at it. We thus relegate God to a second-rate position and elevate ourselves to a place of superiority.

It is presumptuous for us to take any one of God's laws and decide not to obey it. It is not possible for someone to say "No, Lord." "Lord" means master, owner, king. How can we refuse the man who owns all? At whatever point we have said, "No, Lord," we have tried to be God in our lives.

One of the games Christians play is the game of averages. If we average keeping four out of six laws, we feel that we aren't doing too badly. But on the other two points we are saying that God doesn't matter. That is why there is so much frustration and unhappiness among Christians. If there is any place in our lives where God has commanded us to do something and we have refused to do it, we are ridiculing and mocking God's standard. "Don't be misled; remember that you can't ignore God and get away with it: a man will always reap just the kind of crop he sows" (Galatians 6:7).

James is specifically speaking here about one who claims to love his brother and then criticizes him. We are not to do that, but the principle also applies to all of God's laws, in every area of our lives.

"If thou judge the law, thou art not a doer of the law, but a judge." In other words, we don't obey the law, we just tell others what they ought to do. We apply it as we see fit. But God's law is not given to us for our approval or opinion. God is not going to give us a law to decide whether or not we want to keep it. It is to be kept! And whenever we violate God's laws, we violate a principle, and that will cause chaos and confusion to come into our lives.

James goes on to say that there is only one lawgiver who is able to save and to destroy. He is Lord of life and Lord of death.

In the Greek language, one way of emphasizing the point was the position of the words in the sentence. The word appearing first in the sentence received more emphasis. In the question, "Who art thou that judgest another?" (KJV) the emphasis is upon "thou." "Who are *you?* What presumption could possibly be in your heart to cause you to judge another, to play God with someone else's life?"

There are two very good reasons why we cannot pass judgment. The first is we lack perfect information. We do not know all the facts. We only see what is done, not the reason for doing it. Only God possesses all of the facts.

Second, we lack personal integrity. We are guilty also. What kind of trial would it be that let someone already judged "guilty" pass judgment on another? We are all guilty and cannot pass judgment on another. " 'Well,' you may be saying, 'what terrible people you have been talking about!' But wait a minute! You are just as bad. When you say they are wicked and should be punished, you are talking about yourselves, for you do these very things" (Romans 2:1).

The truth of the matter is that whenever we speak evil against someone else, we are speaking our own judgment as well. One day the Pharisees wanted to stone a woman who was guilty of immorality. Jesus said, "Whoever is not guilty can cast the first stone." What can we criticize someone for that we ourselves are not guilty of? We think because we have not murdered or committed immorality we are not guilty, but have we ever hated or lusted?

James is trying to root out that which can destroy harmony and fellowship. "Be kind to each other, tenderhearted, forgiving one another" (Ephesians 4:32). Why? Because we are all likeable? Because we all agree? " . . . just as God has forgiven you because you belong to Christ" (Ephesians 4:32). We can forgive and love on the basis of what Jesus has done in our hearts.

The greatest thing in the world is what God does between people to build love, fellowship, and friendship. God has worked in our lives and hearts to create a genuine love. God takes us with all our differences and builds a fellowship of harmony and love. Because of the love that has been shed abroad in our hearts through Jesus Christ, we can love each other.

Getting the
Most of Today
James 4:13-17

"LOOK HERE, you people who say, 'Today or tomorrow we
are going to such and such a town, stay there a year, and
open up a profitable business.' How do you know what is
going to happen tomorrow? For the length of your lives is
as uncertain as the morning fog—now you see it; soon it is
gone. What you ought to say is, 'If the Lord wants us to,
we shall live and do this or that.' Otherwise you will be
bragging about your own plans, and such self-confidence
never pleases God. Remember, too, that knowing what is
right to do and then not doing it is sin" (4:13-17).

"Look here" tells us James is making an appeal to reason. It could be translated, "Come now." It reminds us of
Isaiah 1:18, "Come now, and let us reason together, saith
the Lord: though your sins be as scarlet. . . ." Our God is
a reasonable God. This prepares us for the foolishness of
the attitude that is about to be described.

ARROGANCE
"Today or tomorrow we are going to such and such a
town, stay there a year, and open up a profitable business" (4:13). Here is a picture of a man who takes a map,
says where he is going to go, and declares he will make a

profit there. There is nothing wrong with planning, but there is a certain arrogance about it if we make plans without God, if God is of no consequence in our lives. "Today or tomorrow" should read "today *and* tomorrow." This pictures men who plan their whole lives without God. How much that describes modern man today! These men have been honest men, men of good character and reputation, but they left God out.

James describes this spirit of arrogant defiance against God. "How do you know what is going to happen tomorrow?" (4:14). We leave God out of our plans as though we were absolute lords of tomorrow. We live as though we know exactly what is going to happen, as though we were in control. But we don't know what is going to happen tomorrow. "Know" means "to be familiar with or to become acquainted with." Here is a man who is ignorant of the future and yet acts as though he knows it all.

" . . . for what is your life?" (4:14, KJV). What is life to us? Is it eating and drinking, playing, working? James tells us, "For the length of your lives is as uncertain as the morning fog—now you see it; soon it is gone" (4:14). The original language says, *"You* are a vapor." We are like the mist and the fog that shrouds the earth early in the morning, but in a matter of a few moments it has disappeared. As quickly as it came, it was gone.

We appear for a little while and then we vanish away. The moment we are born, we begin to die. Who knows how it shall end? Will it be by disease, decay, disaster? Life is soon spent. Life with all of its relationships is soon passed away. Life was not meant to be lived merely for earthly goals and earthly pursuits. The attitude toward life that says, "I will make *my* plans and I will do what I choose to do" is selfish and inadequate.

In verse 16, James gives the conclusion of that attitude: "Otherwise you will be bragging about your own plans, and such self-confidence never pleases God." "Bragging" means "to glory" or "to pride one's self." It refers to empty claims. We have made our plans without God, decided what we are going to do, where we are going to live, how long we are going to live there, what direction our lives will take—all because we are counting on tomorrow. There is plenty of time to repent and live for God. We are going to have our fun first. We are proud of the empty claims that we make but cannot deliver. Can we add one moment to our lives? Can we add one inch to our height?

Some boasting may be legitimate. We can be proud of what God is doing, and we delight ourselves in his purposes. But the boasting that is described here is condemned as evil. There have been many people who have thought that as long as we do not shake our fists in the face of God and denounce him, we are all right. But James says we are evil if we do not include God in our plans. If we do not let God be a part of our todays, we will find our tomorrows crashing in about us.

ADORATION

Only God holds tomorrow. "What you ought to say is, 'If the Lord wants us to, we shall live to do this or that' " (4:15). The phrase "if the Lord wants us to" immediately unfolds for us the reality of the will and purpose of God. We are not simply victims on the sea of life, tossed by every whim of chance. We are not simply driftwood to be torn and tossed about by the storms that arise. We are children of the King, objects of his love and care. He wants us to walk with him into the future.

"Faith is the substance of things hoped for, the evidence of things not seen" (Hebrews 11:1, KJV). "Substance" is a legal word which means "title deed." By faith we have the title deed to things that are hoped for, title deed to the future. God owns the future. When we come by faith to him, we walk into the future, not in the arrogance of our own self-sufficiency and our own plans, but in the assurance of his presence and provision for us. God is interested in what happens to us and how our lives are used.

What if teenagers don't get out of school? Would they have lived in vain? Young couples often say, "When our children are grown. . . ." What happens if they are not around when their children are grown? Will they have lived in vain? Jesus lived only thirty-three years, a brief period upon the earth. Many young people don't live to graduate from high school. Many parents never see their grandchildren. Many people's lives have been cut off, but God's Word tells us that they did not live in vain. God has a purpose and a plan for each person. Whether we are children or adults, men or women, rich or poor, whatever our status may be, there is a purpose for us right now! The happy person is the one who discovers that purpose.

We know the uncertainty of life, but we don't give up in fear and inactivity. Rather, we praise God and realize that our lives are dependent upon him. Our duty is to understand, acknowledge, and accept his will. This does not prevent us from planning, but we ought to plan with God in mind, knowing that if our plans are to be fulfilled, it will be within the providence of God. We are to look toward the future with a spirit that says, "If it is God's will and purpose, we shall carry it out."

Some have felt that this phrase, "If the Lord will" is something that we always have to say verbally. We have included it frequently in our prayers. But used as a verbal pattern of prayer, it could become nothing more than simply an artificial way of addressing God. It is really a very deep and meaningful acknowledgement of the reality of God and his will and purpose. We are to live in an awareness that our lives are under his inspection. We plan, but we plan with God in mind. We acknowledge that our lives are his, and whatever he wants us to do we will do.

ACTION
"Remember, too, that knowing what is right to do and then not doing it is sin" (4:17). One of the great tragedies in our day has been that we have come to treat lightly sins of omission. We have come to think that it is not nearly as bad if we don't do something as it is if we *do* something.

For instance, few of us have any guilt at all over not witnessing for Christ. We go day after day, week after week and never tell anyone about Christ and never invite someone to be saved, and are not even concerned about it. If we rob someone, we feel guilty. If we get mad, lose our temper, or say a curse word, we feel terrible. But we can go all week and not do what is the most precious thing a Christian could ever do and feel no guilt at all.

We have built an immunity to the things we don't do. But James is saying that there is an action demanded of every child of God. It is not just that we fail to do certain things that are wrong, but do we do the things we are commanded to do? He is not talking about things we don't know to do. "Know" in this passage means "to be acquainted with," "to be responsible for."

There are many of us who have lived in absolute rebellion against the purpose of our God by failing to do what we know he wanted us to do. Some of us know we need to be baptized as believers, and yet we have steadfastly refused to do it. Some of us have known for a long time that we ought to be involved in what God is doing through the church, but we don't do it. The essence of rebellion is to say, "No, God, I won't do it."

It is just as evil and just as wicked not to do something

we know to do as it is to do something that we shouldn't do. The word "wicked" is a very strong word that even in the New Testament is not seen very often. One of the classic places it is used is in the parable of the talents. The man who had ten talents multiplied his talents. The man who had five talents multiplied his. But the man who just had one, being afraid he would lose it, hid it and did nothing with it. He didn't squander it. He did nothing with it, and when he was rebuked Jesus said, "Thou *wicked* servant." We might have called him lazy, disorganized, frightened, but "wicked"? The worst sins of any congregation in America are those things we refuse to do. In our self-righteousness, we arrogantly lift ourselves up against what we *know* to be the will of God in our lives.

In John 9, after Jesus had been talking about judgment and those who were blind to eternal truths, the Pharisees angrily asked Jesus, "Are you saying we are blind?" Jesus replied, "If you were blind, you wouldn't be guilty. But your guilt remains because you claim to know what you are doing" (John 9:40, 41). It is a fearful thing for us to know the will of God and to refuse to do it.

In the book of Revelation there is a challenge to the churches. Jesus says he has put the lampstand in the midst of the churches. The light upon the lampstand represents the proclamation of the gospel to a lost world. To one of the churches, Jesus said, "If you don't repent and do what you know you ought to do, I am going to take the lampstand out of your midst. I am going to remove it. Not because you have done something in great disobedience, but because you have refused to do what you know to do." We must acknowledge God's will, accept it, and obey it. If we refuse to do it, we are living in rebellion against him.

The Futility
of Riches
James 5:1-6

"LOOK HERE, you rich men, now is the time to cry and groan with anguished grief because of all the terrible troubles ahead of you. Your wealth is even now rotting away, and your fine clothes are becoming mere moth-eaten rags. The value of your gold and silver is dropping fast, yet it will stand as evidence against you, and eat your flesh like fire. That is what you have stored up for yourselves, to receive on that coming day of judgment. For listen! Hear the cries of the field workers whom you have cheated of their pay. Their cries have reached the ears of the Lord of Hosts. You have spent your years here on earth having fun, satisfying your every whim, and now your fat hearts are ready for the slaughter. You have condemned and killed good men who had no power to defend themselves against you" (5:1-6).

When we come to the fifth chapter of James, we immediately come to one of the most difficult passages to interpret in the entire Bible. We might wonder how it applies to us who are not rich.

James begins by saying, "Look here." We ran into this same phrase in 4:13. It speaks of impending judgment moving in upon those who hold the particular disposition or attitude that is to be described.

The first problem we have is whether he is talking about rich Christians or rich pagans. He does not differentiate between those who have been saved and those who are not saved. Rather, he is addressing those who possess wealth as a class of people. Most of these of course, would have been outside the fellowship of the church. We find that in these first six verses, he does not use the word "brethren," so apparently he is not speaking to the church. In verse 7 and following "brethren" is used often. There is a change of emphasis.

James does not condemn riches, nor does the Bible anywhere condemn those who have material possessions. Rather, the Bible condemns the ungodly way that people gain their possessions and use them. This passage points out that whatever we possess, we are to possess as stewards. They are not to be abused or misused, but are to be used in a positive way.

Jesus emphasizes the responsibility and the reward, the madness and menace of material riches. The harm comes, not when we possess riches, but when riches possess us. And we don't have to be rich to be possessed by riches. A lot of poor folk are obsessed with material things. James is warning us of the dangers of building our lives on material things, the things we can touch, the treasures of the earth.

Paul told Timothy, "People who long to be rich soon begin to do all kinds of wrong things to get money, things that hurt them and make them evil-minded and finally send them to hell itself. For the love of money is the first step toward all kinds of sin. Some people have even turned away from God because of their love for it, and as a result have pierced themselves with many sorrows" (1 Timothy 6:10). Then Paul admonishes Timothy to a positive commitment to righteousness, faith, godliness, love, patience, meekness, etc. Riches or possessions are given to us to bless us, not to curse us. But when we make them the key aim of life and the receiving of possessions the chief end in life, we sabotage and poison our own lives.

THE DESPAIR OF RICHES

"Look here, you rich men, now is the time to cry and groan with anguished grief because of all the terrible troubles ahead of you" (5:1). James is addressing those who have given their lives to what they could possess physically. They had distorted the purpose of possessions. James warns us of the inevitable result of such an attitude: "cry and groan." These two strong words indicate the frantic terror of those on whom God's judgment has fallen and for whom there is no recourse. We find the same picture in Revelation, where we read of kings and wealthy people who abandon God and then cry for the mountains to cover them up and hide them from the wrath of God. Any person who builds his life only upon the physical things of this life will come to know this kind of despair.

God tells us how to use the possessions we have. Stewardship and faithful sharing of possessions is not a scheme to raise money. It is God's method to raise people and to build character into our lives. If we do not learn how to use that which is entrusted to us, despair will come. We can count on trouble.

THE DESTRUCTION OF RICHES

James describes riches that do not last. "Your wealth is even now rotting away, and your fine clothes are becoming mere moth-eaten rags. The value of your gold and silver is dropping fast, yet it will stand as evidence against you, and eat your flesh like fire" (5:2, 3a).

These phrases describe the three basic kinds of wealth in the ancient world. "Wealth" literally refers to grain. One of the ways of determining wealth in the ancient world was the amount of grain a person could store in his barns. "Rotting" indicates grain that was stored and then spoiled. Another way to measure wealth was in the changes of clothes someone had. Of course, clothes are subject to moths. Then James speaks of gold and silver being ruined. In the ancient world, gold and silver were often buried. If it was left in the ground for a period of time, it would corrode. The picture here is of gold and silver losing its value.

The whole picture of these three basic types of wealth is the picture of wealth unused. God never intended for us not to use the wealth that he gives to us. We are to use it. We are to let God have access to it.

What happens when we don't use what God has given to us? Here is a principle that can apply to our physical talents, our mental and emotional attributes, our possessions, our time, etc. It can apply to everything that we are. What happens when we do not allow God access to what he has given to us? Notice: " . . . it will stand as evidence against you" (5:3). God never intended anything he gave us to be wasted, either by abuse, misuse, or lack of use. Everything he gave, he gave to be used. Jesus said, "For anyone who keeps his life for himself shall lose it; and anyone who loses his life for me shall find it again" (Matthew 16:25). We only really have what we give away, share with other people, and give to the kingdom of God. What we give we receive back.

What happens to our riches, our clothes, our gold and silver is but a symbol of what is happening to our soul.

That wealth that soon slips through our fingers, that we cannot hold on to, is but a symbol of what is happening in our heart. How we use what God has given to us is a direct testimony of what is true in our lives spiritually. If we misuse the things we possess, we are simply showing that there is a basic disorder in our souls.

"Don't be misled; remember that you can't ignore God and get away with it: a man will always reap just the kind of crop he sows!" (Galatians 6:7). We may think we can make fun of God, ignore him, live our lives as we choose, but we are sowing the seeds of our own destruction. We and our riches will perish together.

What do we possess that is not passing away? Are we buying bread today with the salary we made ten years ago? Most of us are buying it with the salary we are going to make next week. Are we doing with our strength what we did when we were young? Most of us find that hill we once ran up easily is now a little harder to climb. Our part is not to try to hang on to what we cannot keep, but to be good stewards of the use of it so that God can use and bless it.

Jesus did not condemn the spirit of acquisition in the hearts of his disciples. They came to him one day and said, "We've given up everything to follow you" (Mark 10:28). Jesus did not shame them for wanting to get something out of it, nor did he tell them they were wrong to want to be rewarded. He told them they would be paid a hundredfold in glory. That is certainly a good return on our investment.

Jesus said we can lay up treasures in heaven. How do we do that? How do we transfer the possessions of earth into eternal securities? We do it by bringing what we possess under the Lordship of Jesus and letting him use it. Our part is to make wise investments of what God has given to us so that it can be paying eternal dividends.

THE DANGER OF RICHES

"That is what you have stored up for yourselves, to receive on that coming day of judgment" (5:3). James is saying, "You have been building the wrong kind of treasure. You ought to have been laying up treasures in heaven, but you have been storing up earthly treasure. It will have no value whatsoever in the day of judgment."

Verse 4 talks about the wrong way to get riches. James is not condemning wealth, but the way wealth is acquired. In this particular instance, these rich men sent workers into their fields to harvest the crops, but after they had worked hard to harvest grain so the rich folk could eat, they refused to pay them. This was fraudulent use of the laborers.

"Their cries have reached the ears of the Lord of Hosts." "Lord of Hosts" is the most majestic title you can find for God in the Old Testament. It speaks of the Almighty God and his sovereign omnipotence. It is a word that applies to the King, the Leader of the armies of heaven. James says, "You have robbed the poor and oppressed those less fortunate than you. You may think their cries have gone unheeded and that they have no champion on earth. But their champion is none other than the Lord God Almighty. He has heard and he will bring justice."

Gaining material wealth in the wrong way will bring the opposition of God upon our lives. God expects us to work hard, with honesty and integrity, to gain in that way what is ours. But we must beware of the danger of selfishness.

"You have spent your years here on earth having fun, satisfying your every whim, and now your fat hearts are ready for the slaughter" (5:5). This verse speaks of luxury and self-indulgence. It is the same picture that Paul paints in 1 Timothy, where he speaks of the luxury-living, high-rolling widow who lives in pleasure and is dead while she lives. This is luxurious, extravagant living with no regard for anyone around us. This description fits the vast majority of people in America, even church people.

" . . . and now your fat hearts are ready for the slaughter." This pictures a steer at the stockyard who is not quite heavy enough to be killed. So they put him in a pen and give him the finest food he could possibly have. That steer is so stupid—he doesn't know he is about to be killed, so he lives only for the pleasure and the cravings that he has. When he gains enough weight, they kill him. That is like the man who takes his possessions, lives as though there were no God and no needs in the world around him, and extravagantly takes in pleasure and possessions with no regard for tomorrow. God says, "You are fattening yourselves for the slaughter." The end of pleasure is grief and death.

"You have condemned and killed good men who had no power to defend themselves against you" (5:6). "Condemned" is a judicial word that speaks of those who would so control the courts that there would be no justice. Because they have controlled the courts by their wealth and have taken away the means of support of a person, they are killing that person just as surely as if they committed murder. The rich long to get rid of those who are a blight upon their conscience; the presence of a godly man will always condemn an ungodly man. Socrates had a friend who was very indulgent, living for pleasure in immorality and extravagance. One day he said to Socrates, "Socrates, I hate you. For every time I see you, you show me what I am." Have you ever wondered why good people seem to suffer at the hand of evil people so much? It is because every good man is a condemnation of every evil man.

Whatever God has given to us, we need to use it. God never gave us anything just to enjoy. We have two great extremes in our day. We have people who live as though their possessions were ends in themselves. They live selfishly, extravagantly, luxuriously. The other extreme is the people who possess great religious knowledge and do not use it. Every bit of knowledge and every bit of understanding God gives us, he gives to us to give away. It is not for us to hoard, but to use. That is how God longs to reach the world.

22
Enduring with Patience
James 5:7-12

"NOW AS FOR YOU, dear brothers who are waiting for the Lord's return, be patient, like a farmer who waits until the autumn for his precious harvest to ripen. Yes, be patient. And take courage, for the coming of the Lord is near. Don't grumble about each other, brothers. Are you yourselves above criticism? For see! The great Judge is coming. He is almost here. (Let him do whatever criticizing must be done.) For examples of patience in suffering, look at the Lord's prophets. We know how happy they are now because they stayed true to him then, even though they suffered greatly for it. Job is an example of a man who continued to trust the Lord in sorrow; from his experiences we can see how the Lord's plan finally ended in good, for he is full of tenderness and mercy. But most of all, dear brothers, do not swear either by heaven or earth or anything else; just say a simple yes or no, so that you will not sin and be condemned for it" (5:7-12).

Beginning in verse 7, we have a shift in emphasis. James is speaking now, not to the rich as a class, but to the fellowship of the faith. Several times in these verses the word "brothers" appears. It is obvious that he is talking now to those who have built their lives upon spiritual things. In these verses James is calling us to a commitment that will not let us give an unworthy response to persecution, pressure, or disappointment. A Christian in the midst of opposition must have patient endurance. We can do that as we realize that if God, a holy God, can be patient with us in the face of the enormity of our sin, how much more can we be patient in the face of whatever opposition may come our way.

James is writing now to people whose outlook is dark. He tells them to keep their eyes on the Lord and emphasizes the return of the Lord. The overriding truth of this passage is that whenever we are under pressure, God is very near to us. God will never let us face the burden alone.

THE EXPECTATION

Remember, James is talking to those whose lives have been filled with opposition and persecution. While it seems as though there is no one to take up their cause or stand by their side, in verse 4 he told them that God himself has heard their cries. So he tells them to be patient in the light of God's commitment to them.

We can be patient, James says, in light of the coming of the Lord. The word for "return" is the word *"parousia,"* which speaks of the nearness and certainty of his coming.

To illustrate his point, James talks about the farmer who plants his crop, cultivates it, and then waits for the harvest. He can do nothing now but simply wait for God to cause the seed to germinate and the plant to grow and to send the rain. Just as the farmer can know the Lord is going to send the rain for the crops, so we can know the Lord is going to send his Son once again. Just as the farmer trusts the final outcome to the Lord who sends the rain, we can trust God for the final outcome of our lives. We can live in confident expectation that he will do what he has promised to do.

"Yes, be patient. And take courage, for the coming of the Lord is near" (5:8). "Take courage" means to strengthen your inner being. How do we do this? Doesn't God have to do it? Not without our willingness. Our strength comes from his Word. "Thy word have I hid in mine heart, that I might not sin against thee" (Psalm 119:11, KJV). Paul says, "Whatsoever is not of faith is sin" (Romans 14:23, KJV), and it is his Word that keeps us trusting him.

". . . for the coming of the Lord is near" (5:8). Every generation of men who have walked with God have lived with an anticipation of his return. He is coming again soon; that is the promise of his Word. We are to live our lives in expectancy of that return. "Yes, dear friends, we are already God's children, right now, and we can't even imagine what it is going to be like later on. But we do know this, that when he comes we will be like him, as a result of seeing him as he really is. And everyone who really believes this will try to stay pure because Christ is pure" (1 John 3:2, 3).

The hope of the coming of Jesus Christ is indeed the hope of the heart of God's children. Titus was instructed to "look for the blessed hope." It is a "lively hope," according to Peter. As we live in the expectancy that he will return, something will happen to our lives and there will be a purity that God will build into us that will equip us to face the pressures that come against us in this life.

If we knew Jesus Christ was coming back today, it would make a profound difference in what we do today. There are acts of obedience and commitments of dedication that we would waste no time doing. If we thought we had only one worship service to attend before the Lord returned, it would make a difference in how we worship. If we lived in the expectancy of the return of Jesus Christ, we would be equipped for the pressures and the trials of life. We are to live in that kind of expectation.

THE ACCUSATION

"Don't grumble about each other, brothers. Are you yourselves above criticism? For see! The great Judge is coming. He is almost here. (Let him do whatever criticizing must be done)" (5:9). Sometimes, when we are bombarded by problems by those outside of the fellowship of our family, our church, or our group of friends, our tempers often get short with each other. Sometimes we take our frustrations out on those closest to us. That is a natural tendency, but James is saying, "Do not let the pressure that is brought to bear on you from outside cause you to be unchristian with each other."

The picture is very clear. Imagine a member of a first-century church being arrested because of his commitment to Christ. Another member is not arrested. It was probably hard for the one who was thrown in jail to have a kind attitude toward the one who was free. James says, "Don't look at someone else and complain because they are not suffering as you are. Don't try to involve others in your misery." Paul said, in speaking about fellowship within the church, "Let your moderation be known to all men" (Philippians 4:5, KJV). "Moderation" means "your gracious attitude." James is pleading for us not to pass judgment on each other.

We are to endure our suffering patiently. If we complain and grumble to the fellowship, then we will receive only the strength the fellowship can offer us. If we lift it up to God, we will receive the provision God has for our lives.

"The great Judge is coming. He is almost here" (5:9). This phrase reminds us of the certainty and swiftness of God's judgment. When God's judgment comes, it will be sudden and there will be no recourse. We ought to so walk with God, so pour his Word into our hearts that we do not respond to the pressures of life as the ungodly do. How do we respond to trials? Don't accuse God. Don't accuse each other. The Judge is almost here.

In verses 10, 11 James gives two illustrations of what he means. First he uses the prophets. They have preached in the name of Christ, they have spoken the name of the Lord, and we are to take them as an example of those who suffered affliction and yet were patient. God put his very words in the prophets' hearts and mouths. In essence, James says, "Surely, if anyone ought to have a good time in life and ought to avoid suffering, the prophets would be the ones. Yet they suffered too."

This is a side of Christianity that we do not like to think about—the suffering side. We like to think that when we are saved, everything is going to be glorious. It is true that we will never be away from the presence and power of God. But we will have problems and difficulties. When we get a new Savior, we also get a new enemy. The prophets illustrate patience in suffering. "Patience" means "longsuffering," "long-tempered." They were willing to bear injury without retaliation.

James goes on to say, "We count them happy which endure" (5:11, KJV). "Endure" is the same root word as the word translated "patience" in verse 11, though it is a different Greek word from that translated "patience" in verse 10. "You have heard of the endurance of Job." Not "patience," but "endurance." Job really was not very patient if by patient we mean that he never got angry or upset, never complained. Job did all of that. He got furious with his friends. He got irate with his wife. He complained, but never turned loose of his faith in God. He "endured." He kept an invincible faith in God. "Endure" literally means to "remain under." Job remained under the hand of God and under the circumstances God allowed to come to him.

"We can see how the Lord's plan finally ended in good" (5:11b). If we read Job 42, we will discover what God did in giving back to him what had been taken from him. We will see the end of the Lord's plan. In the end, God showed the world that he loved his servant Job, that he had provided for him. He gave back to him all that had been taken from him, and more. Job saw the ultimate purpose God had for his life. We would like to know what is God's purpose and God's intent for our pressure, opposition, persecution. If we will be patient, trusting God, waiting for the harvest time that God will bring in, we will see what the Lord intended. We will know that "all things work together for good to them that love God, to them who are the called according to his purpose" (Romans 8:28, KJV). Job, through his patience, saw "that he is full of tenderness and mercy." "Tenderness" is a word which speaks of compassion and sympathy. "Mercy" just intensifies that and speaks of an abundantly compassionate and sympathetic God.

THE DEMONSTRATION

"But most of all, dear brothers, do not swear either by heaven or earth or anything else; just say a simple yes or no, so that you will not sin and be condemned for it" (5:12). When James says "most of all," he is saying that the most common response of the human heart to problems and difficulties is to say the wrong thing, to use the wrong oath. He is slapping at the Pharisees who swore by everything. They were doing it to confirm that what they were saying was the truth, but it soon became a joke. They took lightly the matter of taking oaths. This has nothing to do with taking a legal oath in a law court. It is a direct command against the flippant use of our words, particularly the name of God, to guarantee the truth of our statement.

One of the great tragedies in our day is that God's name is used as slang. The name of Jesus, our precious Savior, who died in our behalf, who bore untold agony for us, is used as a curse word. The danger is that when we use

God's name in swearing, we are calling God to be a witness to what we are about to say. So we are asking God to give sanction to our lies, to our exaggerations, to our arrogance, to our pride. This is a dangerous thing. If we see a man walking on crutches, we know he has a bad leg. Swearing is an indication of a weak life; it is a feeble attempt to shore up weakness of character!

Let your yes be yes and your no be no. In other words, say what you mean and mean what you say. We need honesty in our speech. When we say something, we should mean it. Today it is hard to get people to say yes or no to anything. They want to ride the fence. Many of us have a hard time making a commitment. We say we have committed our lives to God, but we don't act like it, we don't live like it. He is not relevant to our lives. What we say on Sunday is not what we do on Monday.

"You are neither hot nor cold; I wish you were one or the other! But since you are merely lukewarm, I will spit you out of my mouth!" (Revelation 3:15, 16). If we have said "yes" to Jesus Christ, we should live it.

" . . . so that you will not sin and be condemned for it" (5:12). We are held responsible for what we say or vow. We are dealing with the Lord God Almighty. When he calls us to do something, our response has to be to him.

Prayer for
the Sick
James 5:13-15

23

"Is ANYONE among you suffering? He should keep on
praying about it. And those who have reason to be thankful should continually be singing praises to the Lord. Is
anyone sick? He should call for the elders of the church
and they should pray over him and pour a little oil upon
him, calling on the Lord to heal him. And their prayer, if
offered in faith, will heal him, for the Lord will make him
well; and if his sickness was caused by some sin, the Lord
will forgive him" (5:13-15).

This is one of the most difficult passages in the Bible to
interpret. But being committed to teaching and living the
Word of God, we cannot ignore it.

This passage deals primarily with prayer, not healing. It
speaks not of physical things, but spiritual things. However, it also speaks of physical healing of the sick.

THE CIRCUMSTANCES
"Is anyone among you suffering? He should keep on
praying about it. And those who have reason to be thankful should continually be singing praises to the Lord. Is
anyone sick? He should call for the elders of the church
and they should pray over him" (5:13, 14). In all circum-

stances we are to pray. This is a wonderful reminder to us that nothing in our lives should alienate us from God. There is no circumstance that is too severe for God to handle. "Suffering" is two words in the original language, meaning "to suffer evil" or "to come under personal hardship." That could be misfortune of health, wealth, or whatever. If that is our situation, we should pray.

Whenever there is oppression upon our lives, whenever there is pressure on us, we are to take it to God and let him bear it. God wants to bless us in the midst of it.

"And those who have reason to be thankful..." We have a tendency to remember God when things are not going well and a tendency to forget him when they are going well. Don't do that. When things are going poorly, we are to pray; when things are going well, we are to sing praises. Some suggest that means we are to literally sing the Psalms, a common practice in the early church. But that really does not apply here. The phrase "let him sing psalms" (KJV) comes from a phrase in the Greek language that meant to pluck at a stringed instrument, such as a harp. As it began to change in its connotation, it simply came to mean, "when you are happy, praise the Lord."

We could transpose these phrases: "If any among you is afflicted, let him praise God. If any is merry, let him pray." In both Ephesians and Thessalonians, Paul tells us to give thanks in everything.

"Is anyone sick?" The Greek word for "sick" means "without strength." It refers to a serious illness or injury. Apparently the person is unable to work. If we have an illness or injury that sidelines us, then we are to call for the elders and let them pray over us.

Why do people get sick? Some say all sickness is the direct result of personal sin. Actually, there are at least six reasons why people get sick. First, there are psychological reasons. If our best statistics are accurate, well over 50 percent of the people in hospitals are there not because they have a real illness, but because of a psychosomatic, self-induced illness.

Another reason is a violation of a natural or physical law. If we fall out of a tree, we may break our arm. That is a violation of the physical law of gravity. The same could be applied to many of the serious illnesses such as cancer, heart attacks, etc. If our bodies knowingly or unknowingly violate a natural law, then disease, accident, and decay are the natural results.

Sickness sometimes comes because God wants to demonstrate his power. John 9 tells of a man born blind. When Jesus was asked whose sin caused the blindness, the man or his parents, Jesus said, "Neither one of them. This man is blind in order that the glory and the power of God might be demonstrated."

Closely associated is a fourth reason for sickness. We find in 2 Corinthians 12 that sickness is sometimes given to demonstrate the grace of God. The Apostle Paul had a "thorn in the flesh" (2 Corinthians 12:7), a physical handicap of some kind. Three times he asked God to heal him of it and finally God said, "My grace is sufficient." Some physical illnesses or weaknesses are given to us in order to reveal the grace of God.

Some illnesses come to us because of the attack of Satan. The book of Job makes this clear.

In the sixth place, some illnesses are caused by sin, though most illnesses are not in this category. In 1 Corinthians 11 Paul tells us some believers had observed the Lord's supper in an unworthy manner; i.e., with unconfessed sins, "For this cause many are weak and sickly" (1 Corinthians 11:30, KJV).

THE COMMAND

If we are sick, we are first to call for the elders of the church. That is a command for us. And the elders are commanded to pray over us. "Elder" speaks of the official ministers of the church, the spiritual leaders. We are not to get sick and then complain that no one cares and comes to see us. We are commanded to call the elders and tell them we are sick. We as a people have a responsibility to inform those who lead us of the needs we have.

The elders are then to "pray over him and pour a little oil upon him, calling on the Lord to heal him. And their prayer, if offered in faith, will heal him, for the Lord will make him well" (5:14b, 15).

First, notice that the elders are to "pray over him." They are not to just pray at home, but are to go to the person and pray by his side. That prayer will bring encouragement as well as the physical healing.

" . . . and pour a little oil upon him, calling on the Lord to heal him." The anointing with oil is one of the most difficult parts of this passage to understand. There are many different interpretations. Some say that the oil in ancient times was a "cure-all," it was a balm for soreness. The Good Samaritan, when he came to the man who was beaten, poured oil over his wounds. It was a common practice to place oil upon an injury or on the place of pain. So some feel this means we are to pray and do everything we can physically. That is *not* what it means! We ought to use doctors and medicine and hospitals, but that is not the point of this passage. The elders are not physicians, so they would scarcely be called on to practice medicine. The anointing of oil cannot be accepted as a medicinal use of oil.

Others say this refers to the gift of healing. There is no question that the spiritual gift of healing operated in New Testament times. But there is no mention of a special gift here. It would be unlikely all of the elders of the church would have the gift of healing.

Others believe that the oil is a ceremonial symbol, evidence of our faith in the presence of the Holy Spirit and a sign of a miraculous cure. It is symbolic of the Holy Spirit. There is some truth to that, but it is not the full answer.

Some would say that the anointing of oil was just for the period of the apostles, and we are not to do this anymore. That may or may not be true. The passage does not actually say that.

Others say the anointing of oil would not work unless the sickness was the result of sin. The Roman Catholic sacrament of extreme unction is based on this verse.

The passage also does not mean that everyone who is going to be healed has to be anointed with oil. In Mark 7 and John 9, Jesus healed blind men, one time by putting saliva on the eyelid and another time by putting clay on the eyes. He did not use oil. Other times, he did not use anything at all.

Some say we will be automatically healed if we call the elders and have them anoint us with oil. We must be very careful to avoid latching on to a magic formula in our search for the miraculous. That is not God's way of doing things.

If this means we are to literally anoint with oil, we have some problems. For example, there has never been a time in history when the church has obeyed that command. It seems as though at some time the church universally would have practiced this with everyone who is sick, but it never has.

The second problem is that there are many instances where people have been anointed with oil and prayed over and they died. Why? We must remember that the emphasis is not upon the oil, but upon the power of the Lord. Notice it says, " . . . anointing him with oil in the name of the Lord" (KJV).

Those who believe this refers to the gift of healing could be partly right, because there was a period of time in the apostolic church when healing seemed to be the rule rather than the exception. Obviously this was not true

throughout the whole New Testament period because
within ten years the Apostle Paul writes of leaving Trophi-
mus ill in Melitus. Instead of raising him up, he left him
sick. He also talks in Philippians about Epaphroditus
being "sick unto death" instead of talking about God's
healing him. Finally, at length he was raised up, but came
to the point of death rather than being healed immediately. Paul himself prayed for his own healing and did
not receive it (2 Corinthians 12:7-11). Today healing is not
the norm. This verse is not referring to a formula that if
repeated will automatically produce healing.

THE CONCLUSION
The most satisfying view is that this passage means to
pray, knowing assuredly what God's will is. If we look in
verses 16-18, we find that Elijah prayed earnestly that it
might not rain and it didn't rain for three and one half
years. Then he prayed again and it rained. If we refer to
the Old Testament, we find that Elijah did not pray that it
not rain or that it would rain until God had already told
him that he was not going to let it rain or that he was going
to let it rain. He announced what God was going to do
after God told him what he was going to do.

The prayer of faith is not something that man can produce, but is something God gives to us. The prayer of faith
is a prayer that God gives when he has already announced
that healing is to take place. Whether we use oil, touch
them by laying hands upon them, or simply lift our voices
to heaven and ask God for healing, the prayer of faith
comes after God has given assurance that it will be
answered.

" . . . for the Lord will make him well; and if his sickness was caused by some sin, the Lord will forgive him"
(5:15). When we pray according to the will of God, and

God wills it, there will be restoration to health. If the person dies, we may know that it was God's perfect plan.

Whatever else this passage means, it means that there is no circumstance in which we cannot call upon the Lord. There is no experience from which we cannot reach out for his help. What do we need today? Are we discouraged? We need only to ask God to encourage us and lift our spirits. We have only to ask our pastor, our staff, the deacons, etc. to pray for our encouragement. Do we find that we are afraid of doing what God wants us to do or of taking a stand for God? Then ask God for courage. Is it forgiveness we need? Ask God. Whatever we need, in all circumstances we are to pray and praise God.

24
Effective
Prayer
James 5:16-18

"ADMIT YOUR FAULTS to one another and pray for each other so that you may be healed. The earnest prayer of a righteous man has great power and wonderful results. Elijah was as completely human as we are, and yet when he prayed earnestly that no rain would fall, none fell for the next three and one half years! Then he prayed again, this time that it would rain, and down it poured and the grass turned green and the gardens began to grow again" (5:16-18).

INTERCESSION
As we look at the passage of Scripture, it falls into two divisions. The first is intercession (5:16). Whenever a church neglects prayer, that church ceases to move under the power of God. Whenever prayer is not a real experience on the part of the child of God, that child of God lives a barren, fruitless, helpless life. Prayer is absolutely essential.

"Confess your faults one to another, and pray one for another, that ye may be healed" (5:16, KJV). These three elements must be taken together. If we are not going to pray for each other, we had better not confess to each other.

James is not talking about a general confession before the church. Confession is a very personal and intimate thing. It deals with the deep problems in our lives. Someone has said that "confession is the vomit of the soul." Indeed, it ought to be.

"Confession" in the original language comes from a Greek word meaning "to say the same thing" or "to agree with." When we confess sin to God, we are agreeing with God's assessment of our lives. We say the same thing God says to us.

Understanding this helps us to understand what our confession to each other is to be. I can't confess something to you that you don't know about. We are not saying the same thing. By the very usage of the word, my confession must agree with the one who is aware of it. We are to confess that which has built a barrier in our fellowship. If we are to have powerful praying, bold intercession before the throne of grace, we need to be of one heart and soul together, with nothing between us.

"Confess your faults one to another" (KJV). "Fault" is a word which implies offenses against brethren. It is not the word for "sins." Our intercession is to begin with our confession one to another, then continue by praying. If we are not going to pray for each other, we ought not to confess to each other, because it can be misused by Satan.

The greatest unused power in the world is the power of believing prayer, prayer that is linked to the omnipotence of God. Praying one for another is the key to what God wants to do in our lives. It is hard to be mad at someone we are praying for. It is hard to be unkind or cynical toward someone we are praying for. If we pour our hearts out in prayer, one for the other, we will find that God will build a bond of love, strength, and fellowship.

" . . . that you may be healed." The healing spoken of in these verses is primarily physical healing. Certainly there is spiritual healing involved, too, because he has already spoken about the forgiveness of sin. The context deals primarily with physical healing. When one is physically healed, his heart repentant and having confessed sins to God and his fellowman, God moves in power to bring the touch of the supernatural life at whatever point the need may exist. As we abide by what he has instructed us to do, we will find healing—emotionally, physically, spiritually, and in every way.

"The earnest prayer of a righteous man has great power and wonderful results" (5:16b). "Earnest" is the word from which we get our word "energy." In the New Testament, this word almost always speaks of God doing the work. It is as though James was saying, "If you are going to have power in prayer, your prayer needs the purposes and power of God himself." The Apostle Paul said, "And we will never stop thanking God for this: that when we preached to you, you didn't think of the words we spoke as being just our own, but you accepted what we said as the very Word of God—which, of course, it was—and it changed your lives when you believed it" (1 Thessalonians 2:13). The phrase "changed your lives" is the same word translated here in James as "earnest."

There are three things we need to notice about prayer. First of all, we see that it is prayer from a righteous man that we are talking about. Some interpret this to mean a person who is saved, for a saved person has appropriated the righteousness of Christ. Jesus, who knew no sin, became sin for us that we might be made the righteousness of God (2 Corinthians 5:21). But this is not what James is saying.

The word "righteous" is to be taken in a practical sense. James is saying that if we have faith, our lives will prove it. A man whose life is a holy life, whose life is consumed with the desire to love and serve God, who walks with and lives for God, will have power in prayer. We have no power in prayer if we have no righteousness in life.

The second thing to notice about prayer is that it is an earnest, energetic prayer, a prayer of enthusiasm, a dynamic prayer. Our praying is to be thoroughly serious as we approach a holy God with our requests.

The Psalmist said, "He would not have listened if I had not confessed my sins" (Psalm 66:18). And the prophet Isaiah said, "Listen now! The Lord isn't too weak to save you. And he isn't getting deaf! He can hear you when you call! But the trouble is that your sins have cut you off from God. Because of sin he has turned his face away from you and will not listen anymore" (Isaiah 59:1, 2).

Notice what happens when we pray as righteous persons, who are committed and obedient to God, with energy and zeal; our prayer "has great power and wonderful results" (5:15). Power does not lie in prayer, but in the Savior. It is God who works and energizes and moves.

ILLUSTRATION

James uses Elijah to illustrate what he means. "Elijah was as completely human as we are, and yet when he prayed earnestly that no rain would fall, none fell for the next three and one half years! Then he prayed again, this time that it *would* rain, and down it poured and the grass turned green and the gardens began to grow again" (5:17, 18).

It is interesting that the prophet prayed for rain. Then he prayed that it wouldn't rain, as an illustration of God's power. This tells us that we can pray about anything; there is nothing that God is not interested in. Whatever is a concern to us is a concern to God. God is interested in everything about our lives: what we do, where we live, what we wear, where we work, what we eat. There is nothing too little to talk to God about.

The second thing this passage tells us is that common

folks can pray. Elijah was a man "as completely human as we are." To the Jew, Elijah was a superman! He walked so closely with God that when he got ready to die, he didn't die. God just took him home. The Jews praised and loved Elijah because of his superspiritual relationship to God. Of course he had power in prayer! He was a spiritual giant, they thought.

But notice that he was a man as completely human as we are. "Completely human" is a phrase that means that he suffered under the same nature as ours. He was subject to the same limitations that we are. He was tempted just as we are tempted. He was liable to commit the same sins that we are. Elijah was no superhero. But when Elijah prayed, God responded.

God is in the business of answering prayers for folks just like us—folks who are tempted, who make wrong choices and wrong decisions, who are subject to the same nature as all mankind. We have access to God; we are priests before him.

We can go into his presence just as surely as Elijah. He was a prophet, but he was not perfect. He had weaknesses. He was haunted by temptation and by Satan. He got depressed and discouraged. After he confronted the 450 prophets of Baal and they were consumed by fire falling from heaven, Jezebel told him she was going to kill him, and he believed her and ran off and hid. He told God, "Lord, I am the only one left who loves you." God said, "No, you are wrong. There are many thousands who have not bowed their knee to Baal. You are not alone. You just think you are." He was tired, depressed, discouraged. He had the same frustrations that we do. All of us can pray, and God will answer our prayers.

Notice that he prayed "earnestly." He really prayed. Praying earnestly means really praying, really talking to God, really committing ourselves to God, really communicating with God. Elijah meant business when he prayed. And that man, because of his sincerity and obedience to God, laid hold of the power of an eternal God.

If we look in 1 Kings at the historical setting of this prayer of Elijah's, we find that Elijah prayed after God had told him it would not rain. Then he prayed that it would rain after God told him that it would rain. His prayer was simply cooperating with the revealed will of God.

25 Turning Sinners to God
James 5:19, 20

"DEAR BROTHERS, if anyone has slipped away from God and no longer trusts the Lord, and someone helps him understand the Truth again, that person who brings him back to God will have saved a wandering soul from death, bringing about the forgiveness of his many sins" (5:19, 20).

Some believe that this passage refers not to Christian brethren, but to Jewish brethren. The use of the word "brothers" by James is a much broader use many times than that of the Apostle Paul. When Paul uses "brothers," he always is referring to fellow-Christians. Some feel James is talking about those who are his brethren in the flesh, lost Jews, and the church is to win them to Christ.

Others believe that "brothers" refers to the church, and those that err from the truth are lost sinners. Consequently, the admonition is to the church to witness to the lost, so they can be saved.

Yet others believe he is not talking about converting one for the first time, but that he is talking about a backslider, one who has fallen away from a close walk with the Lord and is now a rebel against God. If we bring back one who is wayward, one who is wandering from the Lord, then the blessings of verse 20 do come to our lives.

I confess that I do not know what is the true interpretation, though I do not believe that it refers to Jewish brethren. It is possible that he is using brethren to refer to the church and that it is an admonition for us in the church to win the lost. This view solves the problem of interpreting "saving a soul from death" because "death" here means literal death. But if we take that view, we have difficulty interpreting what he means by "if any of *you* do err" (KJV). Does "you" refer to the Christian or the lost? The best way to interpret seems to be that it refers to a backslider.

The key word is the word "brothers." It is used about fifteen times in the epistle of James. When he is comforting them, he refers to them as brothers. When he is instructing them or challenging them, he does it as a brother. He is speaking here to those in fellowship in the church. So he says, "Brethren, if any of you in the fellowship of the church has slipped away from God. . . ."

A SUBTLE DANGER

"Slipped away" is a word that means "to wander, to go astray, to move about aimlessly as though lost." It speaks of one who may once have known the way, but now is aimlessly wandering about. Certainly that fits the description of a backslider, one who has wandered away from his commitment to Christ. In Matthew 18:12 James twice uses the same Greek word to describe the one sheep that had gone astray.

We never backslide suddenly. Slowly and over a period of time it begins to happen until ultimately it becomes a condition of backsliding. It is never a crisis where we plunge headlong into evil. We do it a little at a time.

In the New Testament, there are over and again such words as "beware," "watch," "be diligent" that warn us of the danger of slipping away. The writer of Hebrews says we must be diligent or we will let the things we have heard and received slip from us (Hebrews 2:1). The great danger in the Christian life is that of drifting. A Christian who falls into sin is a Christian who has been careless in many little things, thus making a great sin possible.

Simon Peter told Jesus he would never deny him. He really thought he was saying the truth. But the one thing that Simon Peter did not realize was that over a period of time he had been drifting from his relationship to the Lord; it had become Simon Peter-centered instead of Jesus-centered. He was, I am sure, the most surprised one when he heard himself cursing and denying Jesus. It was almost as though he were listening to someone else.

In the New Testament, the word "truth" either means a system of doctrine or a system of conduct. It is either something we believe or something we do. John 3:21 and 1 John 1:6 both speak of "doing the truth." When James talks about wandering away from the truth, he could be saying that we have denied proper doctrine, we have refused to keep a deep conviction about truth. Or it could mean that we have begun to live and conduct ourselves in a way that denies what we say we believe. It really means both. If we do not believe the right things, it will soon show up in the way we live.

A SUBLIME DUTY

"That person who brings him back to God will have saved a wandering soul from death" (5:20). James is talking about the most precious privilege and the greatest responsibility that lies upon the shoulders of every believer. We have a responsibility, all of us, to convert or "save" the one who has wandered away. "Saved" is a combination of two Greek words which mean "to turn back." We must turn one back to the way he had been walking, back to the way he had been living. This is the same word that

Jesus used when he told Simon Peter, "I have pleaded in prayer for you that your faith should not completely fail. So when you have repented and turned to me again, strengthen and build up the faith of your brothers" (Luke 22:32). It is the sublime duty of every child of God to strengthen and convert those who have wandered away from the Lord.

" . . . that person who brings him back to God will have saved a wandering soul from death, bringing about the forgiveness of his many sins" (5:20). James does not say how we are to do this. But from the context, we have to believe that intercessory prayer has a great deal to do with it. God moves in people's lives as we pray for them.

This much is clear: we have a responsibility to help draw back those who have strayed from the truth. We are to function as a family. When one hurts, all hurt.

I would also point out that James is looking at this matter from man's side, not God's. Obviously, *we* cannot convert anyone. We cannot turn back someone else. Remember, James is not a theologian. He talks about practical Christian living. What he says here is that from man's standpoint, we must get involved and touch the lives of these people. Of course, it is God who will do it through us. But we have a responsibility to give God the opportunity to use us to speak to the hearts of others.

" . . . will have saved a wandering soul from death." What does James mean? There is a strong possibility that this refers to physical death. One of the important themes of the New Testament is sin "unto death," when a Christian becomes so reprobate and so rebellious against God that God has to physically take his life so that he can no longer be used by Satan as an embarrassment and a source of harm to the cause of Christ. James could be saying that a Christian who is brought back to a commitment to Christ is saved from the judgment of God in physical death. A Christian who is reprobate is in danger.

I also believe, however, that death in the New and Old Testaments is often spoken of as an atmosphere in which we live, an atmosphere of despair, guilt, and depression. It may well be saying here that one who is converted from the error of his ways is one who is saved from a living death, a life of waste and emptiness. A Christian away from God is the most miserable person in the world; a Christian who is not living for God is the most unhappy person on earth. The quickest way to unhappiness is to be a compromising, backsliding Christian.

" . . . bringing about the forgiveness of his many sins." The question here is, whose sin is he referring to? Is he speaking of the one who is doing the converting? That is not consistent with the testimony of Scripture. When a sinner is restored, *his* sins are covered. In Hebrews 8:12 and Hebrews 10:16, 17, God says, "I am going to forgive their sins and remember them no more." "Blessed is the man whose sins are covered" (Psalm 32:1). Certainly when a man is restored to fellowship, his life is no longer dominated by the evil that once existed in his life. When he is converted, his soul is saved from death, physical or living. We do not have to live on the basis of our sin and rebellion. We can have our sins covered by the grace of God. The sins of the erring brother are covered when he is converted.

With that rather startling statement, James abruptly stops, to lay stress upon the importance of what he has been saying. From beginning to end, James has been a practical epistle. He has been telling us how to live, how to relate to each other. He has been telling us how to use our tongues, attitudes, thoughts. He has been telling us how to relate to God and to others around us. He has been telling us what our responsibility as children of God really is. Very abruptly he stops, as though to say, "That's all. Now get to it." He ends abruptly with a clarion call for faithful obedience to the will of God in our lives.